november KNITS

INSPIRED DESIGNS *for* CHANGING SEASONS

Kate Gagnon Osborn
Courtney Kelley

INTERWEAVE
Interweave.com

EDITOR *Ann Budd*

TECHNICAL EDITOR *Kristen TenDyke*

ART DIRECTOR *Liz Quan*

PHOTOGRAPHER *Joe Hancock*

PHOTO STYLIST *Carol Beaver*

HAIR AND MAKEUP *Kathy MacKay*

COVER & INTERIOR DESIGN *Julia Boyles*

ILLUSTRATION *Gayle Ford*

PRODUCTION *Katherine Jackson*

Interweave Press LLC
201 East Fourth Street
Loveland, CO 80537
interweave.com

Printed in China by C&C Offset

Library of Congress
Cataloging-in-Publication Data

Osborn, Kate Gagnon.

November knits : inspired designs for
changing seasons / Kate Gagnon Osborn,
Courtney Kelley.

pages cm

Includes index.

ISBN 978-1-59668-439-3 (pbk.)

1. Knitting--Patterns. 2. Women's cloth-
ing. I. Kelley, Courtney. II. Title.

TT825.O83 2012

746.43'2--dc23

2012009823

10 9 8 7 6 5 4 3 2 1

IN GRATITUDE

We would like to extend our grateful and never-ending thanks to the staff at Interweave for enthusiastically supporting us in making this second book a reality.

We owe specific thanks to Anne Merrow for starting us off with patient and practical advice and suggestions that ensured our proposal was enticing and irresistible and to Ann Budd, our (once again) phenomenal editor, who was patient, kind, understanding, and supportive through every step of the process—even as we threw a few curve balls her way. To our tech editor, photographers, models, stylists, and graphic designers, thank you for making this book beautiful and flawless. We could not have done it without you.

A special thank-you goes to our families who continue to wholeheartedly support us on our crazy knitting adventure. They were behind us 150% from the beginning, and their support means the world to us. And, once again, we owe everything to Iain and Daphne, founders of the Fibre Company, for supporting us unconditionally and for giving us freedom to make all the decisions for Fibre Company and Kelbourne Woolens. We are forever grateful for their trust and enthusiasm.

Thanks also go to the yarn companies who generously provided yarn for the projects in this book. Poring through color cards, picking yarns and colors, matching themes, and imagining the beautiful finished product was an exciting and rewarding experience. We are grateful for their support in making the sample garments possible.

Last, but not least, we give thanks and gratitude to the talented, hard-working, and creative knitters who contributed original designs to this book. It was an absolute pleasure to work with each of you, and we hope you are as grateful to be a part of *November Knits* and happy with the end result as we are.

Happy Knitting!

✳ KATE & COURTNEY ✳

CONTENTS

INTRODUCTION

Classic, comfortable, practical, elegant, and understated. These are just a few words that come to mind when we think of our favorite knitwear.

When coming up with ideas for a follow-up to *Vintage Modern Knits*, we knew we wanted to curate a collection of knitwear that would inspire readers. Our aim was to include designs that are hardwearing, warm, and cozy, as well as clever in their construction. We wanted a collection, cohesive in its whole but varied in its content, which would provide the knitter with a multitude of options, colors, shapes, techniques, and styles. The idea for "curating" a collection of designs by some of our favorite established and up-and-coming designers not only provided us with the opportunity to work with a group of people whose designs we know and love, but also to amass a collection of knits that fulfilled our goals of creating a book that will appeal to a wide variety of knitters.

The title *November Knits* evokes the essence of fall and early winter—a time for friends and family to come together and celebrate. With that in mind, we imagined three chapters, each reminiscent of times of togetherness and each representing its own type of knitting techniques. The first chapter, Farm Hands,

is a rustic collection of hardwearing and comfortable garments that are as stylish and aesthetically pleasing as they are practical. The designs in this chapter focus on texture—cables, knit-and-purl combinations, and high-definition stitch variations—all in deep earthy autumn tones of colorful leaves on a crisp fall day. The second chapter, Ivy League, is a classic New England–inspired collection of warm, stylish, and colorful garments meant to be layered on both the inside and out. These designs utilize multiple color techniques—including Fair Isle, stranded colorwork, and stripes—in a palette of bright primaries that provide a welcome pop of color on a cloudy day. The third and final chapter, Southern Comfort, appeals to our feminine side and is a collection of knits in cool vintage-inspired colors evocative of fall in the deep South. The main focus of this collection is decorative embellishment through lace or beads. The designs are lovely and timeless.

We invite you to enjoy whatever autumn brings
your way with these comforting designs.

FARM HANDS

Fall on the farm inspires nesting, hard work in preparation for winter, and taking time to enjoy the crisp outdoors and the crackle of leaves underfoot while harvesting the final bounty from a summer garden. Designed with the idea of working on a ranch or farm, walking in the woods, or sitting around a fire after an afternoon of chopping wood, the projects in this chapter are hardwearing, practical, and useful. The color palette is reminiscent of earthy fall tones—deep maple reds, forest greens, and plenty of shades of brown. Each garment is relatively easy and satisfying to execute with minimal seaming. A pair of warm and soft cabled leg warmers out of a minimally processed yarn in a gorgeous leafy green, a textured jacket with beautiful closures, and a pair of cabled mittens knitted at a tight gauge for optimum warmth and strength are just a few of the projects in this chapter that are sure to prepare you for a real—or imagined—day on the farm.

FINISHED SIZE

About 32 (35½, 39, 42¾, 46¼, 49¾, 53¼, 57)" (81.5 [90, 99, 108.5, 117.5, 126.5, 135, 145] cm) bust/chest circumference.

Pullover shown measures 46¼" (117.5 cm).

YARN

Worsted weight (#4 Medium).

Shown here: Manos del Uruguay Wool Clasica Naturals (100% wool; 138 yd [126 m]/100 g): #701 brown heather, 7 (7, 8, 9, 10, 11, 11, 12) skeins.

NEEDLES

Size U.S. 7 (4.5 mm): 16" and 24" (40 and 60 cm) circular (cir) and set of 4 or 5 double-pointed (dpn).

Adjust needle size if necessary to obtain the correct gauge.

NOTIONS

Smooth waste yarn of comparable gauge for provisional cast-on; markers (m), one of which is a unique color to mark beginning of round; stitch holders; tapestry needle.

GAUGE

18 sts and 24 rnds = 4" (10 cm) according to patt rep in Yoke chart, worked in rnds.

BARNWOOD PULLOVER

DESIGNED BY *Grace Anna Farrow*

The turning of the leaves and crispness of the air in late autumn heralds the return of sweater season. When it is still too early to pull out the winter coat you'll wear for the next few months, you'll want to turn to an easy, comfy sweater. This pullover is completely reversible—the front and back are identical and, if you're careful about joining new yarns, it can be worn inside out as well. Tuck your chin into the cozy turtleneck as you go out and enjoy the last of the autumn sunshine before your winter hibernation.

Stitch Guide

K2, P2 Rib (multiple of 4 sts)
ALL RNDS: *K1, p2, k1; rep from *.

Upper Body

Neck

Loosely CO 64 (64, 64, 80, 80, 80, 96, 96) sts. Place marker (pm) of unique color and join for working in rnds, being careful not to twist sts.

Work in k2, p2 rib (see Stitch Guide) until piece measures 4″ (10 cm) from CO, or desired length.

Yoke

SET-UP RND: Maintaining rib patt, work 20 (20, 20, 28, 28, 28, 36, 36) sts for front, pm, work 12 sts for left sleeve, pm, work 20 (20, 20, 28, 28, 28, 36, 36) sts for back, pm, work 12 sts for right sleeve.

Beg with Rnd 1, work Yoke chart (see page 15), working the necessary number of patt reps between each set of markers. Cont in patt as established through Rnd 38 (42, 46, 48, 48, 48, 48, 48) of chart, then work 0 (0, 0, 0, 8, 10, 12, 16) more rnds to end with Rnd 38 (42, 46, 48, 8, 10, 12, 16)—216 (232, 248, 272, 304, 312, 336, 352) sts total; 50 (54, 58, 60, 68, 70, 72, 76) sts for each sleeve, 58 (62, 66, 76, 84, 86, 96, 100) sts each for front and back.

Divide for Armholes

Keeping in pattern, work 58 (62, 66, 76, 84, 86, 96, 100) sts for front, place next 50 (54, 58, 60, 68, 70, 72, 76) sts for left sleeve onto holder, use a provisional method (see Glossary) to CO 14 (18, 22, 20, 20, 26, 24, 28) sts, work 58 (62, 66, 76, 84, 86, 96, 100) sts for back, place next 50 (54, 58, 60, 68, 70,

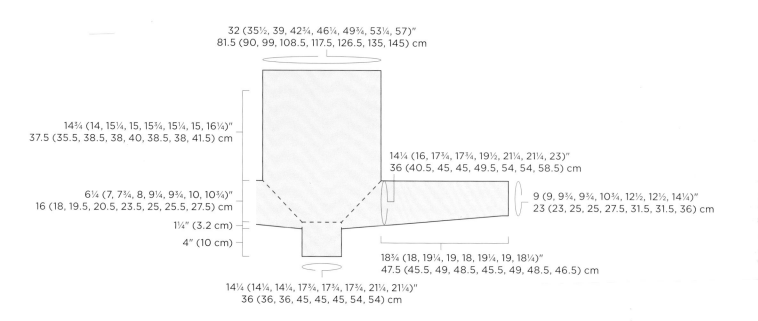

32 (35½, 39, 42¾, 46¼, 49¾, 53¼, 57)"
81.5 (90, 99, 108.5, 117.5, 126.5, 135, 145) cm

14¾ (14, 15¼, 15, 15¾, 15¼, 15, 16¼)"
37.5 (35.5, 38.5, 38, 40, 38.5, 38, 41.5) cm

14¼ (16, 17¾, 17¾, 19½, 21¼, 21¼, 23)"
36 (40.5, 45, 45, 49.5, 54, 54, 58.5) cm

6¼ (7, 7¾, 8, 9¼, 9¾, 10, 10¾)"
16 (18, 19.5, 20.5, 23.5, 25, 25.5, 27.5) cm

9 (9, 9¾, 9¾, 10¾, 12½, 12½, 14¼)"
23 (23, 25, 25, 27.5, 31.5, 31.5, 36) cm

1¼" (3.2 cm)

4" (10 cm)

18¾ (18, 19¼, 19, 18, 19¼, 19, 18¼)"
47.5 (45.5, 49, 48.5, 45.5, 49, 48.5, 46.5) cm

14¼ (14¼, 14¼, 17¾, 17¾, 17¾, 21¼, 21¼)"
36 (36, 36, 45, 45, 45, 54, 54) cm

72, 76) sts for right sleeve onto holder, use a provisional method to CO 14 (18, 22, 20, 20, 26, 24, 28) sts as before—144 (160, 176, 192, 208, 224, 240, 256) sts rem.

Lower Body

Cont in patt as established until piece measures about 12¾ (12, 13¼, 13, 13¾, 13¼, 13, 14¼)" (32.5 [30.5, 33.5, 33, 35, 33.5, 33, 36] cm) from dividing rnd, or about 2" (5 cm) less than desired total length, ending with Rnd 6 or 18 of patt.

Work in k2, p2 rib aligning knit and purl sts with existing patt, for 2" (5 cm).

Loosely BO all sts in patt.

Sleeves

Place 50 (54, 58, 60, 68, 70, 72, 76) held sts sts onto 2 or 3 dpns. Carefully remove waste yarn from provisional CO and place the 14

(18, 22, 20, 20, 26, 24, 28) exposed sts onto another dpn and *at the same time* pm in center of these exposed sts for beg of rnd—64 (72, 80, 80, 88, 96, 96, 104) sts total.

Keeping in patt as established, work 4 rnds even.

DEC RND: Ssk or ssp (see Glossary) as necessary to maintain patt, work as established to last 2 sts, k2tog or p2tog as necessary to maintain patt—2 sts dec'd.

Work 7 (5, 4, 4, 4, 3, 3, 3) rnds even in patt.

Rep the last 8 (6, 5, 5, 5, 4, 4, 4) rnds 11 (15, 17, 17, 19, 19, 19, 19) times—40 (40, 44, 44, 48, 56, 56, 64) sts rem. Cont in patt until piece measures about 16¾ (16, 17¼, 17, 16, 17¼, 17, 16¼)" (42.5 [40.5, 44, 43, 40.5, 44, 43, 41.5] cm) from pick-up rnd, or 2" (5 cm) less than desired total length, ending with Rnd 6 or 18 of patt.

Work in k2, p2 rib, aligning knit and purl sts with existing patt, for 2" (5 cm).

Loosely BO all sts in patt.

Finishing

Weave in loose ends. Block to measurements.

YOKE

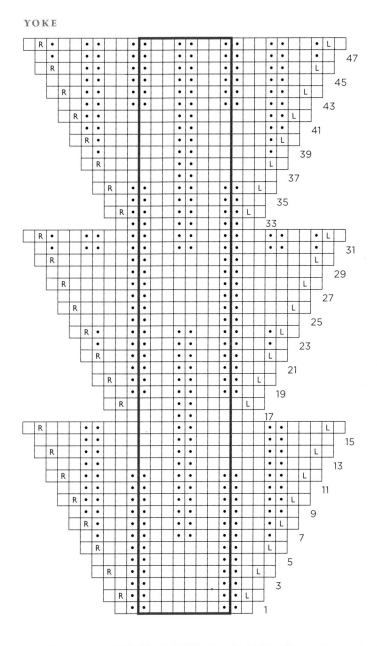

knit

• purl

L M1L

R M1R

■ pattern repeat

Barnwood Pullover

15

FINISHED SIZE

About 10½" (26.5 cm) circumference at widest point, unstretched, 9¼" (23.5 cm) circumference at narrowest point, unstretched, and 13¾" (35 cm) long.

Leg warmers will stretch to accommodate calves from 10" to 15" (25.5 to 38 cm) in circumference.

YARN

Fingering weight (#1 Super Fine).

Shown here: Imperial Stock Ranch Tracie (100% wool; 450 yd [411 m]/4 oz): osprey, 1 skein.

NEEDLES

Size U.S. 4 (3.5 mm): set of 5 double-pointed (dpn).

Adjust needle size if necessary to obtain the correct gauge.

NOTIONS

Markers (m); cable needle (cn); tapestry needle.

GAUGE

26 sts and 34 rnds = 4" (10 cm) in charted patt, worked in rnds.

THISTLE LEG WARMERS

DESIGNED BY *Melissa LaBarre*

I always love the moment when the days shorten and the weather cools so I can add layers of wool to my wardrobe. What better way to extend the wearability of your favorite wardrobe pieces than with a pair of leg warmers? These classic leg warmers combine a simple cable pattern with seed stitch and ribbed edgings. Knitted in a lightweight, rustic 100% wool yarn that is surprisingly strong for its softness, these leg warmers will carry you through many seasons.

Leg Warmer (make 2)

Using the long-tail method (see Glossary), CO 68 sts. Divide sts evenly on 4 dpn, place marker (pm), and join for working in rnds, being careful not to twist sts.

SET-UP RND: *P1, [k1, p1] 6 times, k4; rep from * to end of rnd.

Rep this rnd 20 more times—21 rnds total.

Work Rnds 1–6 of Chart A 7 times—piece measures about 7½" (19 cm) from CO.

Work Rnds 1–6 of Chart B once—60 sts rem.

Work Rnds 1–6 of Chart C 5 times—piece measures about 11¾" (30 cm) from CO.

NEXT RND: *P1, [k1, p1] 5 times, k4; rep from * to end of rnd.

Rep the last rnd 17 more times—18 rnds total.

BO all sts in patt.

Finishing

Weave in loose ends. Gently steam-block to set sts.

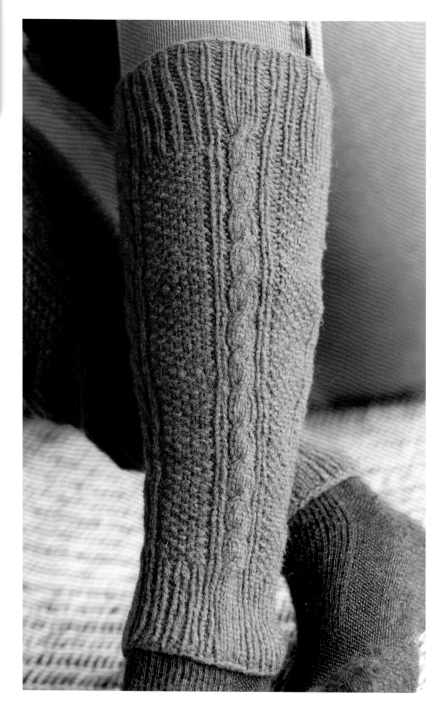

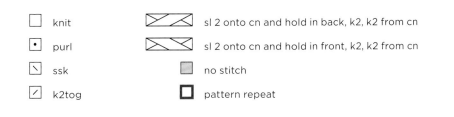

	knit		sl 2 onto cn and hold in back, k2, k2 from cn
•	purl		sl 2 onto cn and hold in front, k2, k2 from cn
\	ssk		no stitch
/	k2tog		pattern repeat

CHART A

5

3

1

CHART B

5

3

1

CHART C

5

3

1

Thistle

FINISHED SIZE

About 8¾" (22 cm) foot circumference, slightly stretched, 9½" (24 cm) foot length, and 10¼" (26 cm) upper leg circumference.

To fit women's U.S. size 8 to 10 shoe.

YARN

DK weight (#3 Light).

Shown here: Rowan Felted Tweed DK (50% merino wool, 25% alpaca, 25% viscose; 191 yd [175 m]/50 g): #150 rage, 2 balls.

NEEDLES

Leg and foot: size U.S. 4 (3.5 mm): set of 4 or 5 double-pointed (dpn).

Ribbing: size U.S. 3 (3.25 mm): set of 4 or 5 dpn.

Adjust needle size if necessary to obtain the correct gauge.

NOTIONS

Markers (m); cable needle (cn); tapestry needle.

GAUGE

24 sts and 36 rnds = 4" (10 cm) in St st on larger needles, worked in rnds.

28 sts in cable patt = 3½" (9 cm) on larger needles, worked in rnds.

McIntosh BOOT SOCKS

DESIGNED BY *Jennifer Burke*

The cables in these socks remind me of windswept, winding roads—perfect for an afternoon of "leaf-peeping" in the countryside. The alpaca content in the Felted Tweed yarn softens the look of the cables and seed stitch without compromising stitch definition or texture. The legs are tapered along the sides in the seed-stitch panels so that the cable panel remains intact. The result is a streamlined look with a perfect fit!

Stitch Guide

Seed Stitch: (multiple of 2 sts)

RND 1: *P1, k1; rep from *.

RND 2: *K1, p1; rep from *.

Rep Rnds 1 and 2 for patt.

Leg

With smaller needles, CO 76 sts. Divide sts on 3 or 4 dpn, place marker (pm), and join for working in rnds, being careful not to twist sts.

Work in k2, p2 rib until piece measures 2½" (6.5 cm) from CO.

Change to larger needles.

SET-UP RND: Work Rnd 1 of Cable chart (see page 25) over 28 sts, pm, work 10 sts in seed st (see Stitch Guide), pm, work Rnd 1 of Cable chart over 28 sts, pm, work 10 sts in seed st.

Keeping in patt and slipping markers (sl m) when you come to them, work through Rnd 15 of chart.

DEC RND: (Rnd 16 of chart) *Work 28 sts as charted, k2tog or p2tog as necessary to maintain patt, work in seed st to 2 sts before m, ssk or ssp (see Glossary) as necessary to maintain patt; rep from * once—4 sts dec'd.

Work Rnds 17–20 of chart.

Rep the last 20 rnds 3 more times, working decs on each rep of Rnd 16 and ending the last rep of the last rnd 1 st before end-of-rnd m—60 sts rem (2 seed sts between each set of markers); piece measures about 11½" (29 cm) from CO.

Heel

Beg with last st from previous rnd, work 30 sts for heel as foll: K1, k1tbl, p2, k1, ssk, [k1, p1] 2 times, k1, p2tog, k2, ssp, [k1, p1] 2 times, k1, k2tog, k1, p2, k1tbl, k1—26 sts rem for heel flap; rem 30 sts will be worked later for instep.

Heel Flap

Work 26 heel sts back and forth in rows as foll:

ROW 1: (WS) Sl 1 purlwise with yarn in front (pwise wyf), p1 through back loop (p1tbl), k2, p2, [k1, p1] 3 times, p2, [p1, k1] 3 times, p2, k2, p1tbl, k1.

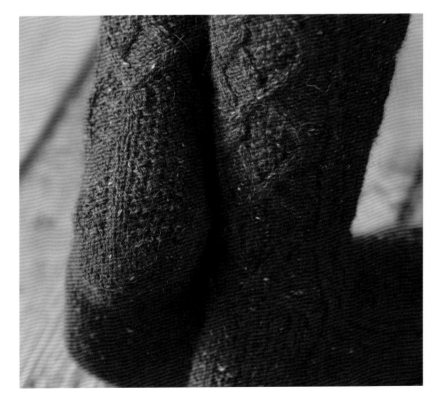

ROW 2: (RS) Sl 1 pwise with yarn in back (wyb), k1tbl, p2, k2, [k1, p1] 3 times, k2, [p1, k1] 3 times, k2, p2, k1tbl, k1.

Rep these 2 rows 11 more times, then work Row 1 once again—26 rows total; 13 slipped chain sts along each selvedge.

Turn Heel

Work short-rows to shape heel as foll:

ROW 1: (RS) Sl 1 pwise wyb, k14, ssk, k1, turn work.

ROW 2: (WS) Sl 1 pwise wyf, p5, p2tog, p1, turn work.

ROW 3: (RS) Sl 1 pwise wyb, knit to 1 st before gap made on previous row, ssk, k1, turn work.

ROW 4: (WS) Sl 1 pwise wyf, purl to 1 st before gap made on previous row, p2tog, p1, turn work.

Rep Rows 3 and 4 until all sts have been worked, ending with a WS row—16 sts rem.

Gussets

With RS facing, k8, pm for new beg of rnd, k8, pick up and knit 14 sts along side of heel flap (13 heel flap sts plus 1 st in the corner between the flap and instep), pm, p1, k1tbl, p2tog, k2, [p1, k1] 3 times, p1, ssk, k2tog, [p1, k1] 3 times, p1, k2, p2tog, k1tbl, p1, pm, pick up and knit 14 sts along other side of heel flap as before, then knit 8 sts from bottom of foot to end of rnd—70 sts total.

SET-UP RND: K8, k14tbl, p1, k1tbl, p1, k2, [k1, p1] 3 times, k4, [p1, k1] 3 times, k2, p1, k1tbl, p1, k14tbl, k8.

Keeping 7 sts in seed st at each side of instep as established, dec gussets as foll:

RND 1: Knit to 3 sts before m, k2tog, k1, sl m, work patt as established across 26 instep sts, sl m, k1, ssk, knit to end—2 sts dec'd.

RND 2: Work even in patt as established.

Rep these 2 rnds 8 more times—52 sts rem.

Foot

Work even in pattern as established until piece measures about 7½" (19 cm) from back of heel, or about 2" (5 cm) less than desired total length.

Toe

Work all sts in St st as foll:

RND 1: *Knit to 3 sts before m, k2tog, k1, sl m, k1, ssk; rep from * once, then knit to end of rnd—4 sts dec'd.

RND 2: Knit.

Rep these 2 rnds 8 more times—16 sts rem; 8 sts each for instep and bottom of foot.

Place each set of 8 sts onto a separate needle.

Finishing

Cut yarn, leaving a 12" (30.5 cm) tail. Thread tail on a tapestry needle and use the Kitchener st (see Glossary) to graft rem sts tog.

Weave in loose ends. Block lightly if desired.

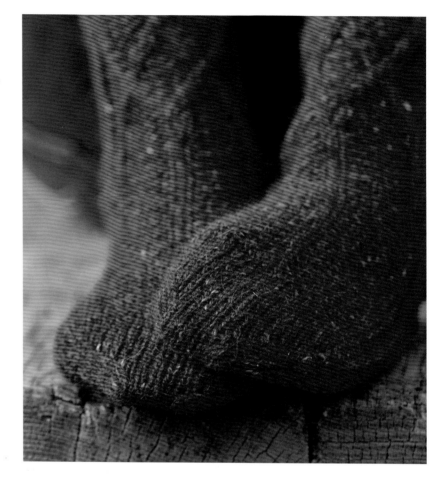

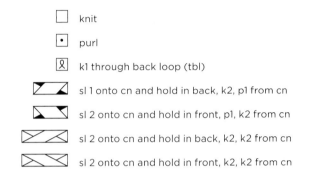

knit

purl

k1 through back loop (tbl)

sl 1 onto cn and hold in back, k2, p1 from cn

sl 2 onto cn and hold in front, p1, k2 from cn

sl 2 onto cn and hold in back, k2, k2 from cn

sl 2 onto cn and hold in front, k2, k2 from cn

CABLE

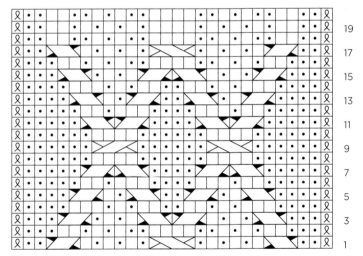

FINISHED SIZE

About 35½ (38, 43½, 46, 51½)"
(90 [96.5, 110.5, 117, 131] cm)
bust/chest circumference, buttoned.

Jacket shown measures 38"
(96.5 cm).

YARN

Chunky weight (#5 Bulky).

Shown here: Berroco Peruvia
Quick (100% Peruvian wool;
103 yd [94 m]/100 g): #9151 bing
cherry, 10 (11, 12, 13, 14) skeins.

NEEDLES

Body and upper sleeve: size
U.S. 11 (8 mm): straight and 3
double-pointed (dpn).

**Collar, lower sleeve, and
pocket linings:** size U.S. 10½
(6.5 mm): 16" (40 cm) or longer
circular (cir) or set of 4 or 5
double-pointed (dpn).

*Adjust needle size if necessary
to obtain the correct gauge.*

NOTIONS

Stitch holders or waste yarn;
tapestry needle; two 6" (15 cm)
toggle closures.

GAUGE

12 sts and 22 rows = 4" (10 cm)
in cartridge belt rib on larger
needles.

BOZEMAN JACKET

DESIGNED BY *Cirilia Rose*

On a recent drive from Providence, Rhode Island, to Seattle, Washington, I passed through Montana and fell in love
with the wide-open craggy landscape. I fell for Montana even
more when I stumbled across the Montana Woolen Shop. It was
full of vintage coats and Shetland sweaters. This enveloping
jacket is inspired by some of the warm and oversized garments
I discovered there. A heavy coat with abbreviated sleeves
might seem counterintuitive, but a little flash of skin lightens
the overall look, and deep pockets provide an instant solution
to any sudden chills.

Stitch Guide

Cartridge Belt Rib
(multiple of 4 sts + 3)

ROW 1: (RS) K3, *sl 1 purlwise with yarn in front (pwise wyf), k3; rep from *.

ROW 2: K1, *sl 1 pwise wyf, k3; rep from * to last 2 sts, sl 1 pwise wyf, k1.

Rep Rows 1 and 2 for patt.

Left I-Cord Edging (panel of 3 sts)

ROW 1: (RS) K3.

ROW 2: Sl 3 pwise wyf.

Rep Rows 1 and 2 for patt.

Right I-Cord Edging (panel of 3 sts)

ROW 1: (RS) Sl 3 pwise wyb.

ROW 2: P3.

Rep Rows 1 and 2 for patt.

I-Cord Bind-Off

With RS facing, *k2, ssk, sl 3 sts just worked pwise to left needle while holding the yarn in back; rep from *.

Back

With larger needles, CO 63 (67, 75, 79, 87) sts. Knit 4 rows. Work in cartridge belt rib patt (see Stitch Guide and chart on page 31) until piece measures 8″ (20.5 cm) from CO, ending with a WS row.

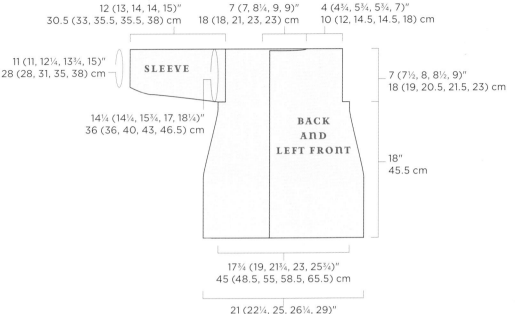

12 (13, 14, 14, 15)″
30.5 (33, 35.5, 35.5, 38) cm

7 (7, 8¼, 9, 9)″
18 (18, 21, 23, 23) cm

4 (4¾, 5¾, 5¾, 7)″
10 (12, 14.5, 14.5, 18) cm

11 (11, 12¼, 13¾, 15)″
28 (28, 31, 35, 38) cm

SLEEVE

7 (7½, 8, 8½, 9)″
18 (19, 20.5, 21.5, 23) cm

14¼ (14¼, 15¾, 17, 18¼)″
36 (36, 40, 43, 46.5) cm

BACK
AND
LEFT FRONT

18″
45.5 cm

17¾ (19, 21¾, 23, 25¾)″
45 (48.5, 55, 58.5, 65.5) cm

21 (22¼, 25, 26¼, 29)″
53.5 (56.5, 63.5, 66.5, 73.5) cm

Shape Sides

DEC ROW: K1, k2tog, work in patt to last 3 sts, ssk, k1—2 sts dec'd.

Knitting the first and last st of every row, work 11 rows even.

Rep the last 12 rows 4 more times—53 (57, 65, 69, 77) sts rem.

Cont even in patt until piece measures 18″ (45.5 cm) from CO, ending with a WS row.

Shape Armholes

BO 4 (4, 3, 4, 4) sts at beg of next 2 rows—45 (49, 59, 61, 69) sts rem. Knitting the first and last st of every row, cont as established until armholes measure 7 (7½, 8, 8½, 9)″ (18 [19, 20.5, 21.5, 23] cm), ending with a WS row.

Shape Shoulders

With RS facing and keeping in patt as established, work 12 (14, 17, 17, 21) sts, then place these sts on a holder or waste yarn, work next 21 (21, 25, 27, 27) sts, then place these sts on another holder or waste yarn, work rem 12 (14, 17, 17, 21) sts, then place these sts on a third holder or waste yarn.

Left Front

With larger needles, CO 42 (46, 46, 50, 54) sts.

ROW 1: (RS) Knit to last 3 sts, work 3 sts in left I-cord edging (see Stitch Guide).

ROW 2: Work 3 sts in left I-cord edging, knit to end.

Rep the last 2 rows once more.

Cont working left I-cord edging at end of RS rows and at beg of WS rows as established, work in cartridge belt rib until piece measures 6″ (15 cm) from CO, ending with a RS row.

Pocket Opening

With WS facing and keeping in patt as established, work 39 (43, 43, 47, 51) sts, then sl last 18 sts just worked onto holder or waste yarn, work in patt to end.

NEXT ROW: (RS) Work 3 sts as established, use the backward-loop method (see Glossary) to CO 18 sts, work in patt to end.

Cont even in patt for 2″ (5 cm), ending with a WS row.

Shape Sides

DEC ROW: (RS) K1, k2tog, work in patt to end—1 st dec'd.

Work 11 rows even.

Rep the last 12 rows 4 more times—37 (41, 41, 45, 49) sts rem.

Cont even in patt until piece measures 18″ (45.5 cm) from CO, ending with a WS row.

Shape Armhole

With RS facing, BO 4 (4, 3, 4, 4) sts, work to end—33 (37, 38, 41, 45) sts rem. Knitting the first st at armhole edge every row, cont in patt as established until armhole measures 7 (7½, 8, 8½, 9)″ (18 [19, 20.5, 21.5, 23] cm), ending with a WS row.

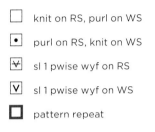

	knit on RS, purl on WS
	purl on RS, knit on WS
	sl 1 pwise wyf on RS
	sl 1 pwise wyf on WS
	pattern repeat

CARTRIDGE BELT RIB

•	V	•	•	V	•
			⩔			1

Shape Neck

Work 12 (14, 17, 17, 21) sts as established, work I-cord BO (see Stitch Guide) until 3 sts rem on right needle tip, BO 3 sts. Place rem sts on a holder or waste yarn for shoulder.

Right Front

With larger needles, CO 42 (46, 46, 50, 54) sts.

ROW 1: (RS) Work 3 sts in right I-cord edging (see Stitch Guide), knit to end.

ROW 2: Knit to last 3 sts, work 3 sts in right I-cord edging.

Rep the last 2 rows once more.

Cont working right I-cord edging at beg of RS rows and at end of WS rows as established, work in cartridge belt rib until piece measures 6″ (15 cm) from CO, ending with a WS row.

Pocket Opening

With RS facing and keeping in patt as established, work 39 (43, 43, 47, 51) sts, then place last 18 sts just worked on a holder or waste yarn, work in patt to end.

NEXT ROW: (WS) Work 3 sts as established, use the backward-loop method to CO 18 sts, work in patt to end.

Cont even in patt for 2″ (5 cm), ending with a WS row.

Shape Sides

DEC ROW: (RS) Work in patt to last 3 sts, ssk, k1—1 st dec'd.

Work 11 rows even.

Rep the last 12 rows 3 more times, then rep dec row once more—37 (41, 41, 45, 49) sts rem.

Cont even in patt until piece measures 18" (45.5 cm) from CO, ending with a RS row.

Shape Armhole

With WS facing, BO 4 (4, 3, 4, 4) sts, work to end—33 (37, 38, 41, 45) sts rem. Knitting the first st at armhole edge every row, cont in patt as established until armhole measures 7 (7½, 8, 8½, 9)" (18 [19, 20.5, 21.5, 23] cm), ending with a WS row.

Shape Neck

With RS facing, work I-cord BO until 15 (17, 20, 20, 24) sts rem, BO 2 sts while working k2, ssk, then place rem 12 (14, 17, 17, 21) sts on a holder or waste yarn.

Join Shoulders

Place 12 (14, 17, 17, 21) held right front shoulder sts on one dpn and corresponding 12 (14, 17, 17, 21) held right back shoulder sts on another dpn. With WS facing tog and using attached tail, use the three-needle method (see Glossary) to BO the sts tog. Rep for left shoulder.

Sleeves

With larger needles, RS facing, and beg at initial armhole BO, pick up and knit 43 (43, 47, 51, 55) sts evenly spaced around armhole edge. Work in cartridge belt rib until piece measures 7½ (8½, 9½, 9½, 10½)" (19 [21.5, 24, 24, 26.5] cm) from CO. Change to smaller needles and cont in patt as established for 1½" (3.8 cm) more, ending after a WS row.

DEC ROW: (RS) K1, k2tog, knit to last 3 sts, ssk, k1—2 sts dec'd.

Cont in garter st, knit 3 rows.

Rep the last 4 rows 4 more times—33 (33, 37, 41, 45) sts rem.

With WS facing, BO all sts.

Finishing

Weave in loose ends. Block pieces to measurements. With yarn threaded on a tapestry needle and beg at cuff edge, sew sleeve seams to underarms. Beg at hem edge, sew side seams to underarms. Lap right front over left front and sew one toggle closure about 1" (2.5 cm) down from neck edge. Sew second toggle closure 2½" (6.5 cm) below the first.

Pocket Lining

Place 18 held pocket sts onto 2 or 3 smaller dpns. With RS facing, join yarn and, with another dpn, pick up and knit 18 sts from CO edge of sts directly above held sts. Place marker (pm), and join for working in rnds—36 sts total.

Knit every rnd until piece measures 5½" (14 cm) from pick-up rnd. Divide sts evenly onto 2 dpns. Hold needles parallel with RS facing tog and use the three-needle method to BO all sts. With yarn threaded on a tapestry needle, tack down corners of pocket lining, if desired.

Collar

With RS facing, smaller cir needle, and beg 1" (2.5 cm) to the right of the right shoulder seam (in I-cord BO of right front), pick up and knit 8 (8, 9, 9, 10) sts along right front neck edge, k21 (21, 25, 27, 27) held back sts, pick up and knit 8 (8, 9, 9, 10) sts along left front neck edge—37 (37, 43, 45, 47) sts total. Working in garter st, work short-rows (see Glossary) as foll:

SHORT-ROW 1: With WS facing, knit to last 3 sts, wrap next st, turn work.

SHORT-ROW 2: With RS facing, knit to last 3 sts, wrap next st, turn work.

NEXT 4 SHORT-ROWS: Knit to 2 sts before last wrapped st, wrap next st, turn work—3 wrapped sts at each side after all short-rows are completed.

NEXT ROW: Knit all sts, hiding wraps by working them tog with their wrapped sts.

Using the I-cord method, BO all sts.

Gently steam-block again, if desired.

FINISHED SIZE

About 34½ (36, 37½, 38½, 40)" (87.5 [91.5, 95.5, 98, 101.5] cm) bust circumference, with ½ (0, ½, 1½, 2)" (1.3 [0, 1.3, 3.8, 5] cm) gap at center front.

Cardigan shown measures 36" (91.5 cm).

YARN

Worsted weight (#4 Medium).

Shown here: Mountain Colors Mountain Goat (55% mohair, 45% wool; 230 yd [210 m/100 g]: olive, 5 (5, 6, 6, 6) skeins.

NEEDLES

Size U.S. 7 (4.5 cm): 32" (80 cm) circular (cir) plus one needle the same size or smaller for joining hem and set of 4 or 5 double-pointed (dpn).

Adjust needle size if necessary to obtain the correct gauge.

NOTIONS

Smooth waste yarn of comparable gauge for provisional cast-on; markers (m); stitch holder or waste yarn; tapestry needle; size G/6 (4 mm) crochet hook.

GAUGE

18 sts and 24 rows = 4" (10 cm) in St st and star patt.

BURDOCK CARDIGAN

DESIGNED BY *Maura Kirk*

This cardigan is inspired by the last green fields to turn fallow; those that are often home to a wide variety of wildflowers, brambles, and thistles that add to the kaleidoscope of colors. The combination of simplicity and elegance—with careful attention to detail—make this sweater an easy layering piece. Hitting just at the hips, the fitted silhouette and open fronts flatter the figure. A stylish alternative to a favorite sweatshirt, this sweater can also be dressed up with the addition of a wide belt at the waist.

Stitch Guide

Star Pattern in Rows
(multiple of 3 sts + 2)

ROW 1: (RS) K1, *yo, k3, use left needle to lift the first of the 3 sts just knitted over the second 2 sts and off the needle; rep from * to last st, k1.

ROW 2: (WS) Purl.

ROW 3: *K3, use left needle to lift the first of the 3 sts just knitted over the second 2 and off the needle, yo; rep from * to last 2 sts, k2.

ROW 4: Purl.

Rep Rows 1–4 for patt.

Star Pattern in Rnds
(multiple of 3 sts)

RND 1: K1, *yo, k3, use left needle to lift the first of the 3 sts just knitted over the second 2 sts and off the needle; rep from * to last 2 sts, yo, k2—1 st inc'd.

RND 2: Knit.

RND 3: *K3, use left needle to lift the first of the 3 sts just knitted over the second 2 and off the needle, yo; rep from * to last 4 sts, k3, use left needle to lift the first of the 3 sts just knitted over the second 2 and off the needle, k1—1 st dec'd.

RND 4: Knit.

Rep Rnds 1–4 for patt.

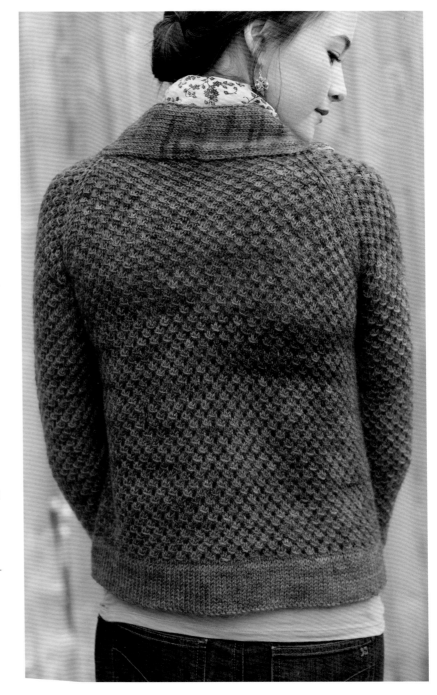

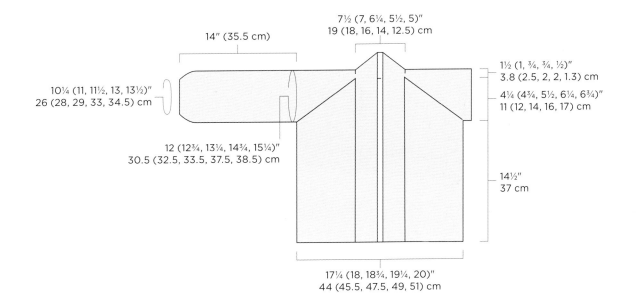

7½ (7, 6¼, 5½, 5)"
19 (18, 16, 14, 12.5) cm

14" (35.5 cm)

1½ (1, ¾, ¾, ½)"
3.8 (2.5, 2, 2, 1.3) cm

10¼ (11, 11½, 13, 13½)"
26 (28, 29, 33, 34.5) cm

4¼ (4¾, 5½, 6¼, 6¾)"
11 (12, 14, 16, 17) cm

12 (12¾, 13¼, 14¾, 15¼)"
30.5 (32.5, 33.5, 37.5, 38.5) cm

14½"
37 cm

17¼ (18, 18¾, 19¼, 20)"
44 (45.5, 47.5, 49, 51) cm

Body

With cir needle, use a provisional method (see Glossary) to CO 153 (162, 171, 180, 189) sts. Do not join. Work even in St st (knit RS rows; purl WS rows) until piece measures 2" (5 cm) from CO for facing, ending with a WS row.

TURNING ROW: (RS) Purl—1 garter ridge on RS.

Work even in St st until piece measures 2" (5 cm) from turning row, ending with a WS row. Using the cable method (see Glossary), CO 15 sts for right front facing—168 (177, 186, 195, 204) sts.

Carefully remove waste yarn from provisional CO and place 153 (162, 171, 180, 189) exposed sts onto spare needle.

JOINING ROW: (RS) K15, fold lower facing to WS along turning row, holding the needles parallel, and join the sts on the 2 needles by working k2tog (1 st from each needle) to end, then use the cable method to CO 15 sts for left front facing—183 (192, 201, 210, 219) sts.

NEXT ROW: (WS) P29 for front band, place marker (pm), purl to last 29 sts, pm, purl to end for other front band.

Cont in patt as foll:

ROW 1: (RS) K14, sl 1 purlwise with yarn in back (pwise wyb) for turning st, k14, slip marker (sl m), work star patt in rows (see Stitch Guide) to m, sl m, k14, sl 1 pwise wyb for turning st, knit to end.

ROW 2: (WS) Purl.

Keeping in patt as established, rep these 2 rows until piece measures about 14½" (37 cm) from turning row, ending with Row 3 of patt.

Divide for Fronts and Back

With WS facing and keeping in patt, work 48 (51, 54, 57, 60) sts for left front, BO 9 sts for left armhole, work 69 (72, 75, 78, 81) sts for back, BO 9 sts for right armhole, work to end for right front—48 (51, 54, 57, 60) sts rem for each front; 69 (72, 75, 78, 81) sts rem for back. Leave sts on needle and set aside. Do not cut yarn.

Sleeves (make 2)

With dpn, use a provisional method to CO 46 (49, 52, 58, 61) sts. Pm and join for working in rnds, being careful not to twist sts. Work even in St st until piece measures 2" (5 cm) from CO.

TURNING RND: (RS) Purl—1 garter ridge on RS.

Work even in St st until piece measures 2" (5 cm) from turning rnd.

Carefully remove waste yarn from provisional CO and place 46 (49, 52, 58, 61) exposed sts on spare needle.

JOINING RND: Fold facing to WS along turning rnd and, holding the needles parallel, join the sts on the two needles by working k2tog (1 st from each needle) to end and *at the same time* inc 8 sts evenly spaced—54 (57, 60, 66, 69) sts.

Work star patt in rnds (see Stitch Guide) until piece measures about 14" (35.5 cm) from turning rnd, ending with Rnd 3 of patt.

NEXT RND: Knit to last 2 sts, BO 6 sts—48 (51, 54, 60, 63) sts rem.

Yoke

JOINING ROW: (RS; Row 1 of patt) Work to band m as established, k1, *yo, k3, lift first of these 3 sts over the second 2 sts and off needle; rep from * to end of front sts, pm, k3, lift first of these 3 sts over the second 2 sts and off needle, *yo, k3 lift first of these 3 sts over the second 2 sts and off needle; rep from last * to end of sleeve sts, pm, k3, lift first of these 3 sts over the second 2 sts and off needle, *yo, k3, lift first of these 3 sts over the second 2 sts and off needle; rep from last * to end of back sts, pm, k3, lift first of these 3 sts over the second 2 sts and off needle, *yo, k3, lift first of these 3 sts over the second 2 sts and off needle; rep from last * to end of sleeve sts, pm, k3, lift first of these 3 sts over the second 2 sts and off needle, *yo, k3, lift

first of these 3 sts over the second 2 sts and off needle; rep from last * to last front st, k1, sl m, work to end as established—257 (272, 287, 308, 323) sts: 48 (51, 54, 57, 60) sts for right front, 47 (50, 53, 59, 62) sts for each sleeve, 68 (71, 74, 77, 80) sts for back, 47 (50, 53, 56, 59) sts for left front.

NEXT ROW: (WS) Purl.

NEXT ROW: Work to band m as established, sl m, k3, lift first of these 3 sts over the second 2 sts and off needle, yo, *k3, lift first of these 3 sts over the second 2 sts and off needle, yo; rep from * to 4 before m, k2, k2tog, sl m, [ssk, k2, yo, *k3, lift first of these 3 sts over the second 2 sts and off needle, yo; rep from last * to 4 before m, k2, k2tog, sl m] 3 times, ssk, k2, yo, *k3, lift first of these 3 sts over the second 2 sts and off needle, yo; rep from last * to last 2 sts, k2—253 (268, 283, 304, 319) sts rem; 47 (50, 53, 56, 59) sts each front; 46 (49, 52, 58, 61) sts each sleeve; 67 (70, 73, 76, 79) sts for back.

NEXT ROW: Purl.

Cont working decs as foll:

ROW 1: (RS) Work to band m as established, sl m, k1, *yo, k3, lift first of these 3 sts over the second 2 sts and off needle; rep from * to 2 sts before raglan m, k2tog, sl m, [ssk, k3, lift first of these 3 sts over the second 2 and off needle, *yo, k3, lift first of these 3 sts over the second 2 sts and off needle; rep from last * to 2 sts before next raglan m, k2tog] 3 times, ssk, k3, lift first of these 3 sts over the second 2 sts and off needle, *yo, k3, lift first of these 3 sts over the second 2 sts and off needle; rep from last * to 1 st before band m, k1, sl m, work to end as established—12 sts dec'd.

ROW 2: Purl.

ROW 3: Work to band m as established, sl m, k3, lift first of these 3 sts over the second 2 sts and off needle, *yo, k3, lift first of these 3 sts over the second 2 sts and off needle; rep from * to 2 sts before raglan m, k2tog, sl m, [ssk, k3, lift first st over second 2 sts and off needle, *yo, k3, lift first of these 3 sts over the second 2 sts and off needle; rep from last * to 2 sts before next raglan m, k2tog] 3 times, ssk, k3, lift first of these 3 sts over the second 2 sts and off needle, *yo, k3, lift first of these 3 sts over the second 2 sts and off needle; rep from last * to 2 sts before band m, yo, k2, sl m, work to end as established—12 sts dec'd.

ROW 4: Purl.

Rep the last 4 rows 3 (4, 5, 6, 7) more times—157 (148, 139, 136, 127) sts rem; 35 sts for each front; 22 (19, 16, 16, 13) sts each sleeve; 43 (40, 37, 34, 31) sts for back.

NEXT ROW: (RS) Work as for Row 1 to last raglan m, ssk, k3, lift first of these 3 sts over the second 2 sts and off needle, k1, sl m, work to end as established—12 sts dec'd.

NEXT ROW: Purl.

NEXT ROW: (RS) Work to band m as established, sl m, k3, lift first of these 3 sts over the second 2 sts and off needle, k2tog, sl m, [ssk, k3, lift the first of these 3 sts over the second 2 sts and off needle, *yo, k3, lift first of these 3 sts over the second 2 sts and off needle; rep from * to 2 sts before next raglan m, k2tog] 3 times, ssk, k2, sl m, work to end as established—12 sts dec'd.

NEXT ROW: Purl.

NEXT ROW: (RS) Work to band m as established, sl m, k3tog, sl m, [ssk, k3, lift first of

these 3 sts over the second 2 sts and off needle, *yo, k3, lift first of these 3 sts over the second 2 sts and off needle; rep from * to 2 sts before next raglan m, k2tog] 3 times, sssk (see Glossary), sl m, work to end as established—120 (111, 102, 99, 90) sts rem; 30 sts for each front; 13 (10, 7, 7, 4) sts each sleeve, 34 (31, 28, 25, 22) for back.

Purl 1 WS row.

With RS facing, work 29 right front sts and place these sts on a holder to work later, BO 62 (53, 44, 41, 32) sts for sleeves and back, work rem 29 left front sts.

Collar Extensions

Work 29 left front sts as foll:

ROW 1: (WS) Purl.

ROW 2: (RS) K2tog, knit to slipped st, sl 1, knit to last 2, ssk—2 sts dec'd.

Rep Rows 1 and 2 until extension measures to center back neck. Place sts on holder.

Return right front sts to working needle and join yarn in preparation to work a WS row. Rep as for left front, but leave sts on needle. Cut yarn, leaving an 18" (45.5 cm) tail.

Finishing

Return 29 held left front collar extension sts to needle and, with tail threaded on tapestry needle, use the Kitchener st (see Glossary) to join sts to right front hem sts. With yarn threaded on a tapestry needle, sew collar extensions along tops of sleeve and back neck.

Fold front hems to WS at turning st and use a whipstitch (see Glossary) to sew in place.

With crochet hook and beg at lower right front edge, work single crochet (see Glossary) along the fold line at center fronts, working into the turning st (i.e., the slipped st) and making sure to crochet together the bottom folded hem opening.

Weave in loose ends. Block to measurements.

FINISHED SIZE

About 8" (20.5 cm) hand circumference and 9½" (24 cm) long, including cuff.

To fit a woman's hand.

YARN

Worsted weight (#4 Medium).

Shown here: Brown Sheep Company Nature Spun Worsted Weight (100% wool; 245 yd [224 m]/100 g): #720W ash, 1 skein.

NEEDLES

Cuff: size U.S. 3 (3.25 mm): set of 4 or 5 double-pointed (dpn).

Hand: size U.S. 6 (4 mm): set of 4 or 5 dpn.

Adjust needle size if necessary to obtain the correct gauge.

NOTIONS

Marker (m); 2 cable needles (cn); tapestry needle; waste yarn.

GAUGE

20 sts and 30 rnds = 4" (10 cm) in St st on larger needles, worked in rnds.

29 sts and 32 rnds = 4" (10 cm) in charted pattern on larger needles, worked in rnds.

PALOMINO MITTENS

DESIGNED BY *Elli Stubenrauch*

Perfect for keeping fingers toasty while raking leaves or doing other autumnal chores, these mittens are knitted from a lovely, yet basic, worsted-weight wool. The texture-rich design features a meandering pattern of traveling twisted stitches and cables that show the yarn to its best advantage. A slightly denser-than-recommended gauge ensures durability and warmth while small details, such as the purled thumb and ribs that extend into the cables, create a refined look to the rustic hard-wearing yarn.

Right Mitten

With smaller needles, CO 48 sts. Divide sts evenly onto 3 or 4 dpn, place marker (pm), and join for working in rnds, being careful not to twist sts.

Cuff

SET-UP RND: [K1 through back loop (k1tbl), p1] 11 times, k2tbl, [p1, k1tbl] 12 times.

Cont in rib as established until piece measures 2″ (5 cm) from CO.

Hand

INC RND: Work Rnd 1 of Right Hand chart (see page 46)—58 sts.

Change to larger dpn. Work Rnds 2–61 of Right Hand chart, inc for thumb beg on Rnd 4 as indicated and place 19 gusset sts on waste yarn holder at beg of Rnd 23— 22 sts rem after Rnd 61.

Cut yarn, leaving an 18″ (45.5 cm) tail.

Transfer first 11 sts to waste yarn holder and transfer rem 11 sts to another yarn holder.

Turn mitten inside out and with WS facing, return each set of 11 held sts to a separate dpn. Using the tail, work the three-needle method (see Glossary) to BO the sts tog.

Thumb

With RS facing, return 19 held gusset sts to dpn. Leaving a long tail, rejoin yarn and pick up and knit 1 st tbl in the gap between thumb sts and hand, p9, k1tbl, p9—20 sts total.

RND 1: [K1tbl, p2tog, p7, M1P (see Glossary)] 2 times.

RND 2: [K1tbl, p9] 2 times.

Rep these 2 rnds 4 more times.

Dec for top of thumb as foll:

DEC RND 1: [K1tbl, p2tog, p2tog, p1, p2tog, p2tog] 2 times—12 sts rem.

DEC RND 2: [K1tbl, p2tog, p1, p2tog] 2 times— 8 sts rem.

DEC RND 3: [K2togtbl, p2tog] 2 times—
4 sts rem.

Cut yarn, leaving an 8" (20.5 cm) tail. Thread
tail on a tapestry needle, draw through rem
sts, pull tight to close hole, and fasten off
on WS.

Left Mitten

With smaller needles, CO 48 sts. Divide sts
evenly onto 3 or 4 dpn, place marker (pm),
and join for working in rnds, being careful
not to twist sts.

Cuff

SET-UP RND: [K1tbl, p1] 12 times, k2tbl, [p1,
k1tbl] 11 times.

Cont in rib as established until piece measures 2" (5 cm) from CO.

Hand

Work as for right mitten, but follow Left
Hand chart (see page 47).

Thumb

Work as for right mitten.

Finishing

With yarn threaded on a tapestry needle,
close gap between thumb and hand.

Weave in loose ends. Block lightly.

⟨knit tbl symbol⟩	knit tbl	⟨P⟩	M1P	⟨cable symbol⟩	sl 1 onto cn and hold in back, k1 tbl, k1 tbl from cn
•	purl	⟨p2tog symbol⟩	p2tog	⟨cable symbol⟩	sl 1 onto cn and hold in front, k1 tbl, k1 tbl from cn
⟨M⟩	M1	⟨gray⟩	no stitch	⟨cable symbol⟩	sl 1 onto cn and hold in back, k1 tbl, p1 from cn
				⟨cable symbol⟩	sl 1 onto cn and hold in front, p1, k1 tbl from cn

RIGHT HAND

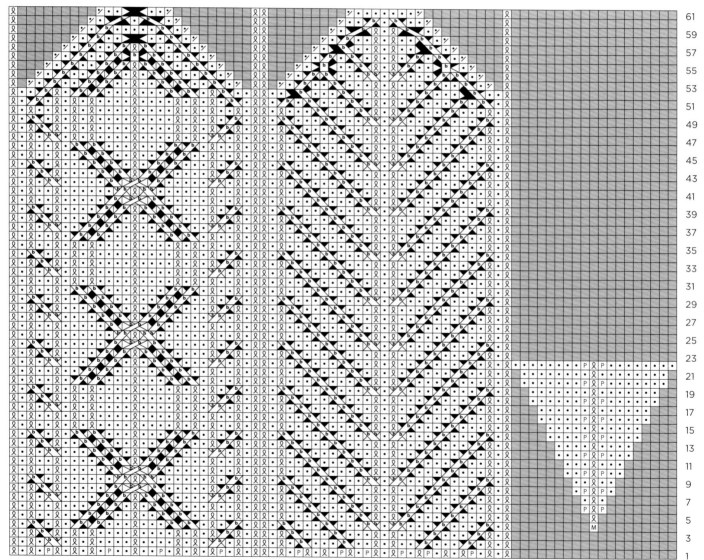

sl 1 onto cn and hold in back, sl 1 onto second cn and hold in back, k1 tbl, k1 tbl from second cn, k1 tbl from first cn

 sl 1 onto cn and hold in front, sl 1 onto second cn and hold in back, k1 tbl, k1 tbl from second cn, k1 tbl from first cn

 sl 1 onto cn and hold in front, p1, move cn to back, k1 tbl, p1 from cn

 sl 1 onto cn and hold in front, sl 1 to second cn and hold in back, p1, k1 tbl from first cn, p1 from second cn

 sl 1 onto cn and hold in front, sl 1 onto second cn and hold in front, p1, move first cn to back, k1 tbl second cn, p1 from first cn

 sl 1 onto cn and hold in back, sl 1 onto second cn and hold in front, p1, k1 tbl from second cn, p1 from first cn

 sl 1 onto cn and hold in back, sl 1 onto second cn and hold in front, p1, p1 from second cn, p1 from first cn

 sl 1 onto cn and hold in front, p2, k1 tbl from cn

sl 2 onto cn and hold in back, k1 tbl, p2 from cn

LEFT HAND

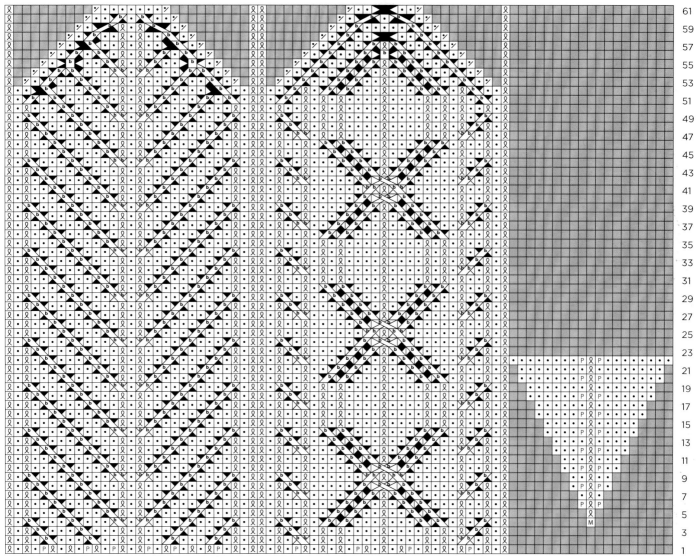

61
59
57
55
53
51
49
47
45
43
41
39
37
35
33
31
29
27
25
23
21
19
17
15
13
11
9
7
5
3
1

FINISHED SIZE

About 33¾ (37¼, 41¼, 45¼, 49¼, 53¼, 57¼, 61¾)" (85.5 [94.5, 105, 115, 125, 135.5, 145.5, 155.5] cm) bust circumference, buttoned with 1" (2.5 cm) overlap.

Coat shown measures 37¼" (94.5 cm).

YARN

Worsted weight (#4 Medium).

Shown here: Green Mountain Spinnery Mountain Mohair (70% wool, 30% yearling mohair; 140 yd [128 m]/2 oz): spice, 6 (7, 8, 9, 10, 11, 12, 13) skeins.

NEEDLES

Body and sleeves: size U.S. 9 (5.5 mm): 24" (60 cm) circular (cir) and set of 5 double-pointed (dpn).

Edging and collar: size U.S. 7 (4.5 mm): 24" (60 cm) cir and set of 5 dpn.

Adjust needle size if necessary to obtain the correct gauge.

NOTIONS

Smooth waste yarn of comparable gauge for provisional cast-on; markers (m); cable needle (cn); stitch holders; tapestry needle; seven (seven, seven, eight, eight, nine, nine, nine) ¾" (2 cm) buttons.

GAUGE

16 sts and 23 rows = 4" (10 cm) in St st on larger needles.

19 sts of Cable and Lace chart = 3¾" (9.5 cm) wide.

MARKET JACKET

DESIGNED BY *Tanis Gray*

This cardigan brings back memories of cold autumn and early winter afternoons spent hiking in the White Mountains of New England while I was growing up. I pushed up my sleeves so I could grab interesting leaves, rocks, and berries to show my dad. The three-quarter-length sleeves in this coat leave your arms and hands free to explore, while the wool/mohair blend provides warmth. The cable-and-lace pattern reminds me of the vegetation on the forest floor, and the heathered yarn, with its golds, reds, and oranges, evokes the colors of changing leaves.

Yoke

With larger cir needle and waste yarn, use a provisional method (see Glossary) to CO 57 (61, 65, 69, 73, 77, 81, 85) sts. Do not join.

RAGLAN SET-UP ROW: (WS) P10 (11, 12, 13, 14, 15, 16, 17) for front, place marker (pm), p9 for sleeve, pm, p19 (21, 23, 25, 27, 29, 31, 33) for back, pm, p9 for sleeve, pm, p10 (11, 12, 13, 14, 15, 16, 17) for front.

PATT SET-UP ROW: (RS) K1 (selvedge st), work first 8 (9, 10, 11, 12, 13, 14, 15) sts of Cable and Lace chart (see page 53) for left front, yo, k1, slip marker (sl m), k1, yo, work center 7 sts of chart for sleeve, yo, k1, sl m, k1, yo, k0 (0, 1, 2, 3, 4, 5, 6), work center 17 (19, 19, 19, 19, 19, 19, 19) sts of chart for back, k0 (0, 1, 2, 3, 4, 5, 6), yo, k1, sl m, k1, yo, work center 7 sts of chart for sleeve, yo, k1, sl m, k1, yo, work last 8 (9, 10, 11, 12, 13, 14, 15) sts of chart for right front, k1 (selvedge st)—8 sts inc'd.

NEXT ROW: (WS) Working inc'd sts into established patt, *p1, work to 1 st before m, p1, slip marker (sl m); rep from * 3 times, work to last st, p1.

INC ROW: (RS) Cont in patt, *work to 1 st before m, yo, k1, sl m, k1, yo; rep from * 3 times, work to end of row—8 sts inc'd.

NOTE: Once 19 sts of chart have been established on each section, work remaining increased sts in St st.

Rep the last 2 rows 23 (25, 27, 29, 31, 33, 35, 37) more times, ending with a RS row—257 (277, 297, 317, 337, 357, 377, 397) sts total; 35 (38, 41, 44, 47, 50, 53, 56) sts for each front, 59 (63, 67, 71, 75, 79, 83, 87) sts for each sleeve, 69 (75, 81, 87, 93, 99, 105, 111) sts for back; piece measures about 8¾ (9½, 10, 10¾, 11½, 12¼, 12¾, 13½)" (22 [24, 25.5, 27.5, 29, 31, 32.5, 34.5] cm) from CO, measured straight down at center back.

Divide for Armholes

With WS facing, *purl to m, place 59 (63, 67, 71, 75, 79, 83, 87) sts on holder for sleeve, CO 2 (3, 5, 7, 9, 11, 13, 15) sts for underarm; rep from * once, purl to end—143 (157, 173, 189, 205, 221, 237, 253) sts rem for body.

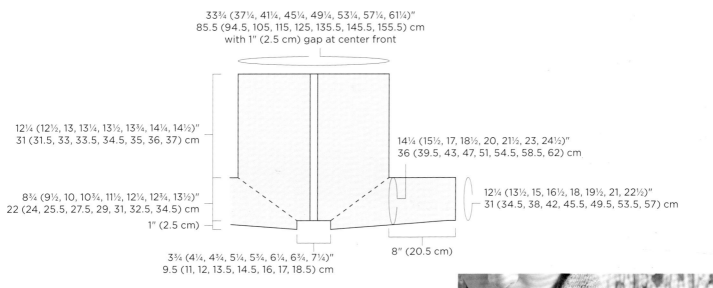

33¾ (37¼, 41¼, 45¼, 49¼, 53¼, 57¼, 61¼)"
85.5 (94.5, 105, 115, 125, 135.5, 145.5, 155.5) cm
with 1" (2.5 cm) gap at center front

12¼ (12½, 13, 13¼, 13½, 13¾, 14¼, 14½)"
31 (31.5, 33, 33.5, 34.5, 35, 36, 37) cm

14¼ (15½, 17, 18½, 20, 21½, 23, 24½)"
36 (39.5, 43, 47, 51, 54.5, 58.5, 62) cm

8¾ (9½, 10, 10¾, 11½, 12¼, 12¾, 13½)"
22 (24, 25.5, 27.5, 29, 31, 32.5, 34.5) cm

1" (2.5 cm)

12¼ (13½, 15, 16½, 18, 19½, 21, 22½)"
31 (34.5, 38, 42, 45.5, 49.5, 53.5, 57) cm

3¾ (4¼, 4¾, 5¼, 5¾, 6¼, 6¾, 7¼)"
9.5 (11, 12, 13.5, 14.5, 16, 17, 18.5) cm

8" (20.5 cm)

Body

Cont in patt until piece measures 11¼ (11½, 12, 12¼, 12½, 12¾, 13¼, 13½)" (28.5 [29, 30.5, 31.5, 32, 32.5, 33.5, 34.5] cm) from underarm CO ending with a WS row.

Change to smaller cir needle and work even in garter st (knit every row) for 1" (2.5 cm). Loosely BO all sts knitwise.

Sleeves

With RS facing, arrange 59 (63, 67, 71, 75, 79, 83, 87) sleeve sts as evenly as possible on 3 larger dpn. With a fourth dpn, pick up and knit 2 (3, 5, 7, 9, 11, 13, 15) sts from underarm and pm as close to the center of these sts as possible—61 (66, 72, 78, 84, 90, 96, 102) sts total. Join for working in rnds.

Cont in patt, work 5 rnds even.

DEC RND: K2tog, work in patt to last 2 sts, ssk—2 sts dec'd.

Work 5 rnds even. Rep the last 6 rnds 5 more times—49 (54, 60, 66, 72, 78, 84, 90) sts rem.

Cont even in patt until piece measures 7" (18 cm) from pick-up rnd, ending with an even numbered rnd of chart.

Change to smaller dpn and work even in garter st for 1" (2.5 cm).

Loosely BO all sts knitwise.

Finishing
Block to measurements.

Buttonband
With RS facing, smaller cir needle, and beg at upper left front edge, pick up and knit 61 (63, 67, 70, 72, 75, 79, 81) sts evenly spaced along left front. Knit 8 rows, ending with a RS row. Loosely BO all sts knitwise.

Buttonhole Band
With RS facing, smaller cir needle, and beg at lower right front edge, pick up and knit 61 (63, 67, 70, 72, 75, 79, 81) sts evenly spaced along right front. Knit 3 rows.

BUTTONHOLE ROW: (RS) K3 (4, 3, 3, 4, 5, 3, 4), yo, k2tog, *k7 (7, 8, 7, 7, 6, 7, 7), yo, k2tog; rep from * 5 (5, 5, 6, 6, 7, 7, 7) more times, k2 (3, 2, 3, 4, 2, 3)—7 (7, 7, 8, 8, 9, 9, 9) buttonholes made.

Knit 4 rows even.

Loosely BO all sts knitwise.

Collar
With smaller cir needle, RS facing, and beg at top of buttonhole band, pick up and knit

4 sts from buttonhole band, carefully remove waste yarn from CO row and place 57 (61, 65, 69, 73, 77, 81, 85) exposed sts onto needle and knit across, then pick up and knit 4 sts from button band—65 (69, 73, 77, 81, 85, 89, 93) sts total. Do not join.

Beg with a WS row, work in garter st for 3" (7.5 cm), ending with a RS row.

Loosely BO all sts knitwise.

Weave in loose ends.

Sew buttons to buttonband, opposite buttonholes.

CABLE AND LACE

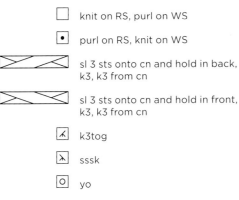

- ☐ knit on RS, purl on WS
- ☐• purl on RS, knit on WS
- ⬚⬚ sl 3 sts onto cn and hold in back, k3, k3 from cn
- ⬚⬚ sl 3 sts onto cn and hold in front, k3, k3 from cn
- 丆 k3tog
- 人 sssk
- O yo

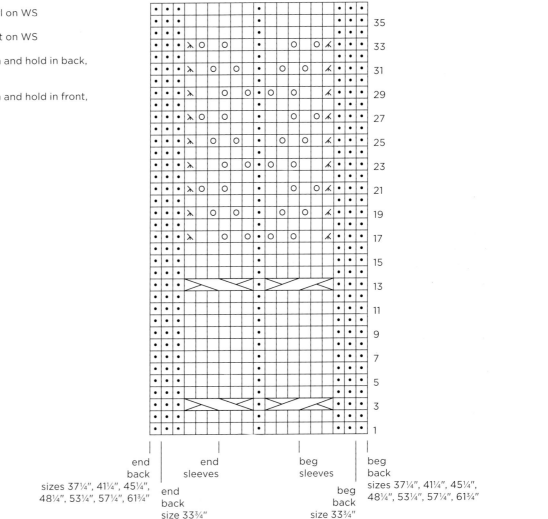

end
back
sizes 37¼", 41¼", 45¼",
48¼", 53¼", 57¼", 61¾"

end
sleeves

beg
sleeves

beg
back
sizes 37¼", 41¼", 45¼",
48¼", 53¼", 57¼", 61¾"

end
back
size 33¾"

beg
back
size 33¾"

IVY LEAGUE

Fall in New England means the last days of the farmer's market, cool evenings in rocking chairs on wraparound porches, L.L.Bean totes filled with thermoses of hot apple cider, final days on the shore, winterizing the boats in preparation for the cold months ahead, and the crisp, clean smell of trees changing their colors. The garments and accessories in this chapter are simultaneously classic and modern and are designed to look as appropriate in the stands of a football game as at a family feast. The color palette—bright blues, greens, and yellows, with neutral shades for balance—evoke the quintessential New England aesthetic. A fitted classic striped sweater knitted out of a gorgeous certified organic wool, a hat-and-mitten set in a graphic maritime-inspired Fair Isle pattern, and a pair of colorwork socks in soft, strong, and hard-wearing hand-dyed yarn are just a few of the garments featured in this chapter. Let them transport you to a beautiful fall New England day.

FINISHED SIZE

About 7½ (8½)" (19 [21.5] cm)
foot circumference and 9½
(10¼)" (24 [26] cm) foot length.

To fit women's U.S. size 6 to 8
(8 to 10) shoe.

YARN

Fingering weight (#1 Super Fine).

Shown here: Lorna's Laces
Shepherd Sock Solid (80% wool,
20% nylon; 430 yd [393 m]/114 g):
#58ns kerfuffle (purple; MC) and
#013 aqua (CC), 1 skein each.

NEEDLES

Size U.S. 1 (2.25 mm): 32" circular (cir) or set of 4 or 5 double-
pointed (dpn).

*Adjust needle size if necessary
to obtain the correct gauge.*

NOTIONS

Smooth contrasting color waste
yarn of comparable gauge for
tubular cast-on; markers (m);
tapestry needle.

GAUGE

38 sts and 39 rnds = 4" (10 cm) in
charted pattern, worked in rnds.

WALDEN POND
SOCKS

DESIGNED BY *Elinor Brown*

Geometric designs in nature have always appealed to the
pragmatist in me. The uncertain movements of rippling water
as leaves fall to the surface always have me grasping to find a
sense of rhythm. The cool blue autumn sky reflected in dark
gray waters is mirrored here in a houndstooth-inspired pattern,
creating the perfect socks to pair with your sensible penny
loafers while you ponder the depths of whatever you see while
strolling through the woods.

Leg

With MC and waste yarn, use the tubular method worked in rnds (see Glossary) to CO 60 (70) sts.

SET-UP RND: *K1, p1; rep from *.

Cont in rib as established until piece measures 2½" (6.5 cm) from CO.

Knit 1 rnd.

INC RND: *K6 (7), M1 (see Glossary); rep from *—70 (80) sts.

Work Rnds 1–10 of Embossed Squares chart 3 times, then work Rnds 1–5 once more.

Heel

Work for your size as foll:

SIZE 7½" ONLY:
With MC and RS facing, *sl 1 knitwise with yarn in back (kwise wyb), k32, k2tog—34 heel sts; rem 35 sts will be worked later for instep.

SIZE 8½" ONLY:
With MC and RS facing, *sl 1 knitwise with yarn in back (kwise wyb), k39—40 heel sts; rem 40 sts will be worked later for instep.

Heel Flap

Work 34 (40) heel sts back and forth in rows as foll:

ROW 1: (WS) Sl 1 purlwise with yarn in front (pwise wyf), purl to end.

ROW 2: (RS) *Sl 1 kwise wyb, k1; rep from *.

Rep these 2 rows 16 more times, then work Row 1 again—36 rows total; 18 slipped chain sts along each selvedge.

Turn Heel

Work short-rows to shape heel as foll:

ROW 1: (RS) Sl 1 kwise wyb, k20 (24), ssk, k1, turn work.

ROW 2: (WS) Sl 1 pwise wyf, p9 (11), p2tog, p1, turn work.

ROW 3: (RS) Sl 1 kwise wyb, knit to 1 st before gap made on previous row, ssk, k1, turn work.

ROW 4: (WS) Sl 1 pwise wyf, purl to 1 st before gap made on previous row, p2tog, p1, turn work.

Rep Rows 3 and 4 until all sts have been worked, ending with a WS row—22 (26) sts rem.

Gussets

With RS facing, sl 1 kwise wyb, knit to end of heel sts, pick up and knit 18 (19) sts along right selvedge of heel flap, pm to indicate new beg of rnd. Join CC.

◨ with MC, knit

⊡ with CC, knit

☐ pattern repeat

EMBOSSED SQUARES

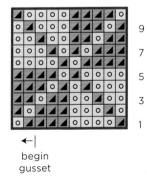

←|
begin gusset

SET-UP RND: Work 34 (39) instep sts in established patt, pm for side of foot, work last instep st in patt, beg where indicated on chart, use colors in patt to pick up and knit 19 (19) sts along other selvedge of heel flap, then cont in patt to 1 st before end of rnd—94 (104) sts total.

RND 1: Knit the last st of the previous rnd tog with the first st of next rnd, work in patt to marker, sl m, ssk, work to end—2 sts dec'd.

RND 2: Work even in patt to last st of rnd (do not work last st).

Rep the last 2 rnds 11 more times—70 (80) sts rem.

Move side of foot marker 1 st to the right.

Foot

Cont even in patt until piece measures about 7½ (8)″ (19 [20.5] cm) from back of heel or 2 (2¼)″ (5 [5.5] cm) less than desired total length, ending with Rnd 5 or 10 of chart.

Cut CC.

Toe

With MC, knit 1 rnd.

Dec as foll:

RND 1: *K1, ssk, knit to 3 sts before m, k2tog, k1, sl m; rep from *—4 sts dec'd.

RND 2: Knit.

Rep the last 2 rnds 3 (5) more times, then rep Rnd 1 only (i.e., dec every rnd) 10 times, ending at side of foot—14 (16) sts rem.

Arrange sts so 7 (8) top-of-foot sts are on one needle and the corresponding 7 (8) bottom-of-foot sts are on a second needle. Cut yarn, leaving an 8" (20.5 cm) tail.

Finishing

With tail threaded on a tapestry needle, use the Kitchener st (see Glossary) to graft sts tog.

Weave in loose ends. Block to smooth out color pattern.

FINISHED SIZE

About 32 (34¾, 36½, 39½, 41¾, 44½, 48½)" (81.5 [88.5, 92.5, 100.5, 106, 113, 123] cm) bust circumference, buttoned.

Cardigan shown measures 34¾" (88.5 cm).

YARN

Worsted weight (#4 Medium).

Shown here: Green Mountain Spinnery Local Color (100% certified organic fine wool; 180 yd [198 m]/56 g): #01 indigo (blue; MC), 5 (5, 6, 6, 6, 7, 8) skeins; #03 fern (green; CC) 2 (2, 3, 3, 3, 3, 3) skeins.

NEEDLES

Body and sleeves: size U.S. 6 (4 mm): straight.

Ribbing: size U.S. 5 (3.75 mm): straight and 24" (60 cm) circular (cir).

Adjust needle size if necessary to obtain the correct gauge.

NOTIONS

Markers (m); stitch holder; tapestry needle; five ⅝" (1.5 cm) buttons.

GAUGE

18 sts and 27 rows = 4" (10 cm) in St st on larger needles.

THAYER STREET CARDIGAN

DESIGNED BY *Melissa Wehrle*

Inspired by school colors, fall sports, and rooting for the home team, this sweater is a modern take on the classic varsity cardigan, sans letter. Stripes are one of the easiest ways to introduce multiple colors in knitting—the combination of different stripe patterns makes them that much more interesting. The two stripe patterns used for the fronts meet at the center back, where they are worked in the intarsia method. Because the stripe patterns change only along the center back, this project is perfect for someone tackling intarsia for the first time.

NOTES

❖ The back panel is worked in stockinette-
stitch intarsia with the little stripe pattern
on the right half and the big stripe pattern
on the left. Each half is worked with separate balls of MC and CC. The yarns are
twisted at the center to prevent holes.

❖ The left front is worked in the big stripe
pattern; the right front is worked in the
little stripe pattern.

Stitch Guide

Little Stripe

ROWS 1 AND 2: MC.

ROWS 3 AND 4: CC.

Rep Rows 1–4 for patt.

Big Stripe

ROWS 1–4: MC.

ROWS 5–8: CC.

Rep Rows 1–8 for patt.

Back

With MC and smaller needles, CO 78 (82, 90,
94, 102, 110, 118) sts.

SET-UP ROW: (WS) P2, *k2, p2; rep from *.

Cont in rib as established until piece measures 1¾" (4.5 cm) from CO, ending with a
WS row.

Change to larger needles and St st.

SET-UP ROW: Work Row 1 of little stripe patt
(see Stitch Guide) across 39 (41, 45, 47, 51,
55, 59) sts, place marker (pm), join a second
ball of MC and work Row 1 of big stripe patt
(see Stitch Guide) across rem 39 (41, 45, 47,
51, 55, 59) sts.

Work 3 more rows in patt, joining CC on each
half when necessary and twisting yarns in
the intarsia method (see sidebar on page 65)
every row at the marker.

Shape Waist

DEC ROW: (RS) Keeping in patt, k1, ssk, work to last 3 sts, k2tog, k1—2 sts dec'd.

Work 5 (7, 7, 7, 5, 5, 7) rows even in patt.

Rep the last 6 (8, 8, 8, 6, 6, 8) rows 1 (4, 4, 4, 3, 2, 2) more time(s), then rep dec row every 8 (0, 0, 0, 8, 8, 10) rows 3 (0, 0, 0, 2, 3, 2) times—68 (72, 80, 84, 90, 98, 108) sts rem.

Work 7 rows even in patt.

INC ROW: (RS) Keeping in patt, k1, M1 (see Glossary), work to last st, M1, k1—2 sts inc'd.

Work 5 (3, 5, 3, 3, 3, 3) rows even.

Rep the last 6 (4, 6, 4, 4, 4, 4) rows 3 (1, 3, 1, 1, 2, 2) more time(s), then rep inc row every 8 (6, 8, 6, 6, 6, 6) rows 2 (5, 2, 5, 5, 4, 4) times—80 (86, 92, 98, 104, 112, 122) sts.

Work even in patt until piece measures 13¾ (14, 14, 14, 14¼, 14¼, 14¼)" (35 [35.5, 35.5, 35.5, 36, 36, 36] cm] from CO, ending with a WS row.

Shape Armholes

Keeping in patt, BO 5 (6, 6, 6, 7, 7, 8) sts at beg of next 2 rows—70 (74, 80, 86, 90, 98, 106) sts rem. Dec 1 st each end of needle every row 2 (3, 3, 3, 3, 5, 7) times, then every RS row 0 (0, 2, 4, 4, 4, 4) times—66 (68, 70, 72, 76, 80, 84) sts rem.

Cont in patt until armholes measure 7¼ (7½, 7¾, 8, 8¼, 8¾, 9¼)" (18.5 [19, 19.5, 20.5, 21, 22, 23.5] cm), ending with a WS row.

Shape Right Neck and Shoulder

With RS facing, BO 5 (5, 5, 5, 6, 6, 7) sts, work 10 (11, 12, 12, 13, 14, 15) sts so there are

---

WORKING INTARSIA

INTARSIA is a method used to work two or more colors at a time without floats across the wrong side of the work. When working in this method, it is important to twist the yarns around each other every time the colors are changed to prevent holes from forming at the color changes. It is also important to maintain consistent tension so the stitches are not distorted at the color boundaries.

For this sweater, the intarsia method is used only along the center back at the boundary between the two stripe patterns. Even though the same color may be used on each half, be sure to twist and change yarns on every row so that each half is worked with separate balls of yarn. Because of this, one ball of each color is used for each stripe pattern—four balls total for the back.

To twist the yarns, work to the color or yarn change, then bring the new yarn up from *under* the yarn just worked. This will catch the yarn just worked at the back of the work and prevent any holes from forming.

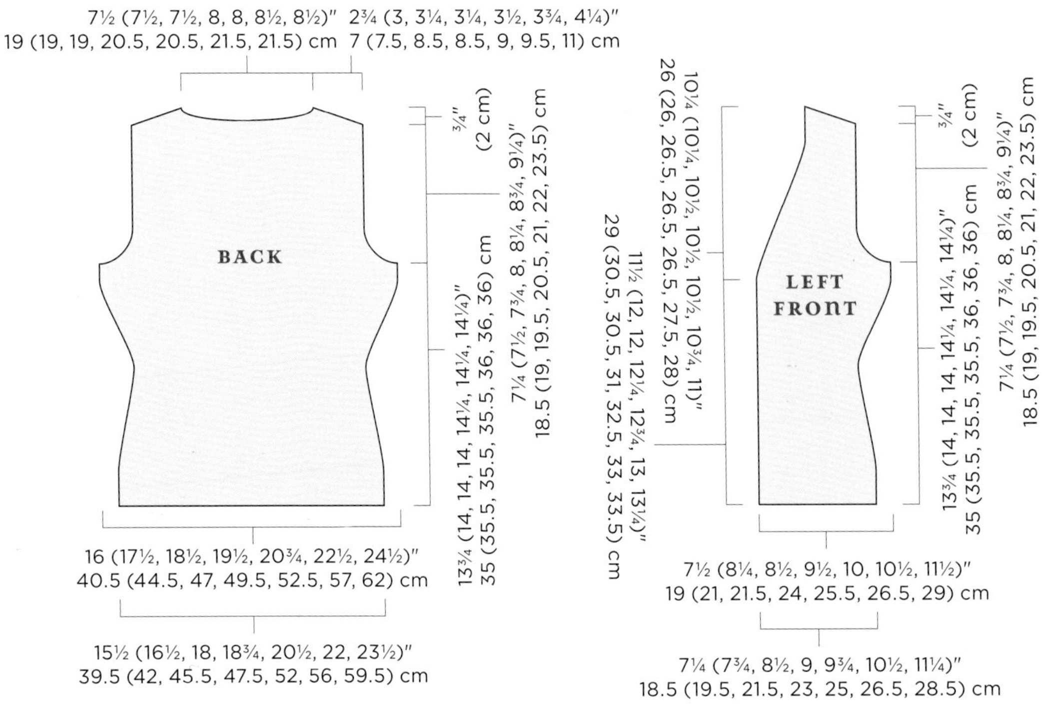
7½ (7½, 7½, 8, 8, 8½, 8½)"
19 (19, 19, 20.5, 20.5, 21.5, 21.5) cm
2¾ (3, 3¼, 3¼, 3½, 3¾, 4¼)"
7 (7.5, 8.5, 8.5, 9, 9.5, 11) cm
¾"
(2 cm)
7¼ (7½, 7¾, 8, 8¼, 8¾, 9¼)"
18.5 (19, 19.5, 20.5, 21, 22, 23.5) cm
BACK
13¾ (14, 14, 14, 14¼, 14¼, 14¼)"
35 (35.5, 35.5, 35.5, 36, 36, 36) cm
16 (17½, 18½, 19½, 20¾, 22½, 24½)"
40.5 (44.5, 47, 49.5, 52.5, 57, 62) cm
15½ (16½, 18, 18¾, 20½, 22, 23½)"
39.5 (42, 45.5, 47.5, 52, 56, 59.5) cm
10¼ (10¼, 10½, 10½, 10½, 10¾, 11)"
26 (26, 26.5, 26.5, 27.5, 28) cm
11½ (12, 12, 12¼, 12¾, 13, 13¼)"
29 (30.5, 30.5, 31, 32.5, 33, 33.5) cm
LEFT FRONT
¾"
(2 cm)
7¼ (7½, 7¾, 8, 8¼, 8¾, 9¼)"
18.5 (19, 19.5, 20.5, 21, 22, 23.5) cm
13¾ (14, 14, 14, 14¼, 14¼, 14¼)"
35 (35.5, 35.5, 35.5, 36, 36, 36) cm
7½ (8¼, 8½, 9½, 10, 10½, 11½)"
19 (21, 21.5, 24, 25.5, 26.5, 29) cm
7¼ (7¾, 8½, 9, 9¾, 10½, 11¼)"
18.5 (19.5, 21.5, 23, 25, 26.5, 28.5) cm

11 (12, 13, 13, 14, 15, 16) sts on right needle tip, then place rem 50 (51, 52, 54, 56, 59, 61) sts on holder.

Work 11 (12, 13, 13, 14, 15, 16) sts for right shoulder as foll:

NEXT ROW: (WS) P2tog, work to end—1 st dec'd.

NEXT ROW: BO 5 (5, 5, 5, 6, 6, 7) sts, work to last 2 sts, k2tog—4 (5, 6, 6, 6, 7, 7) sts rem.

Work 1 WS row even. With RS facing, BO rem 4 (5, 6, 6, 6, 7, 7) sts.

Shape Left Neck and Shoulder

With RS facing, return 50 (51, 52, 54, 56, 59, 61) held sts to needle and join yarn.

With RS still facing, BO 34 (34, 34, 36, 36, 38, 38) sts for neck, work to end—16 (17, 18, 18, 20, 21, 23) sts rem.

NEXT ROW: (WS) BO 5 (5, 5, 5, 6, 6, 7) sts, work to last 2 sts, ssp (see Glossary)—10 (11, 12, 12, 13, 14, 15) sts rem.

NEXT ROW: Ssk, work to end—1 st dec'd.

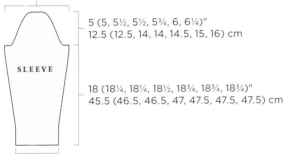

11¼ (11½, 12, 12¾, 13¼, 14½, 16)"
28.5 (29.5, 30.5, 32.5, 33.5, 37, 40.5) cm

5 (5, 5½, 5½, 5¾, 6, 6¼)"
12.5 (12.5, 14, 14, 14.5, 15, 16) cm

SLEEVE

18 (18¼, 18¼, 18½, 18¾, 18¾, 18¾)"
45.5 (46.5, 46.5, 47, 47.5, 47.5, 47.5) cm

8½ (9¼, 9¼, 10, 10, 10¾, 11½)"
21.5 (23.5, 23.5, 25.5, 25.5, 27.5, 29) cm

NEXT ROW: BO 5 (5, 5, 5, 6, 6, 7) sts, work to end of row—4 (5, 6, 6, 6, 7, 7) sts rem.

Work 1 RS row even. BO all sts.

Left Front

With MC and smaller needles, CO 36 (39, 42, 45, 49, 52, 56) sts.

SET-UP ROW: (WS) P0 (1, 0, 0, 0, 0, 0), k0 (2, 2, 1, 1, 0, 0), *p2, k2; rep from * to end of row.

Work in rib as established until piece measures 1¾" (4.5 cm) from CO, ending with a

WS row. Change to larger needles and St st and, beg with Row 1, work big stripe patt for 4 rows, ending with a WS row.

Shape Waist

DEC ROW: (RS) Keeping in patt, k1, ssk, work to end of row—1 st dec'd.

Work 5 (7, 7, 7, 5, 5, 7) rows even. Rep the last 6 (8, 8, 8, 6, 6, 8) rows 1 (4, 4, 4, 3, 2, 2) more time(s), then rep dec row every 8 (0, 0, 0, 8, 8, 10) rows 3 (0, 0, 0, 2, 3, 2) times— 31 (34, 37, 40, 43, 46, 51) sts rem.

Work 7 rows even, ending with a WS row.

NOTE: Neck shaping is introduced while waist shaping is in progress and armhole shaping is introduced while neck shaping is in progress; read all the way through the foll sections before proceeding.

INC ROW: (RS) Keeping in patt, k1, M1, work to end—1 st inc'd.

Work 5 (3, 5, 3, 3, 3) rows even. Rep the last 6 (4, 6, 4, 4, 4) rows 3 (1, 3, 1, 1, 2, 2) more time(s), then rep dec row every 8 (6, 8, 6, 6, 6, 6) rows 2 (5, 2, 5, 5, 4, 4) times.

At the same time when piece measures 11½ (12, 12, 12¼, 12¾, 13, 13¼)" (29 [30.5, 30.5, 31, 32.5, 33, 33.5] cm) from CO, ending with a WS row, shape neck as foll.

Shape Neck

DEC ROW: (RS) Cont waist shaping as established, work to last 3 sts, k2tog, k1—1 st dec'd.

Work 1 row even. Rep the last 2 rows 1 (3, 0, 4, 4, 3, 2) more time(s), then rep dec row every 4 rows 14 (13, 15, 13, 13, 14, 15) time(s).

At the same time when piece measures 13¾ (14, 14, 14, 14¼, 14¼, 14¼)" (35 [35.5, 35.5, 35.5, 36, 36, 36] cm) from CO, ending with a WS row, shape armhole as foll.

Shape Armhole

With RS facing, BO 5 (6, 6, 6, 7, 7, 8) sts, work to end. Work 1 row even. Dec 1 st at armhole edge (beg of RS rows; end of WS rows) every row 2 (3, 3, 3, 3, 5, 7) times, then every RS row 0 (0, 2, 4, 4, 4, 4) times. Cont neck shaping, work in patt until armhole

measures 7¼ (7½, 7¾, 8, 8¼, 8¾, 9¼)" (18.5 [19, 19.5, 20.5, 21, 22, 23.5] cm), ending with a WS row—14 (15, 16, 16, 18, 19, 21) sts rem after all shaping is completed.

Shape Shoulder

At shoulder edge (beg of RS rows), BO 5 (5, 5, 5, 6, 6, 7) sts 2 times, then BO rem 4 (5, 6, 6, 6, 7, 7) sts.

Right Front

With MC and smaller needles, CO 36 (39, 42, 45, 49, 52, 56) sts.

SET-UP ROW: (WS) *K2, p2; rep from * to last 0 (3, 2, 1, 1, 0, 0) st(s), k0 (2, 2, 1, 1, 0, 0), p0 (1, 0, 0, 0, 0, 0).

Work in rib as established until piece measures 1¾" (4.5 cm), ending with a WS row. Change to larger needles and St st and, beg with Row 1, work little stripe patt for 4 rows, ending with a WS row.

Shape Waist

DEC ROW: (RS) Keeping in patt, work to last 3 sts, k2tog, k1—1 st dec'd.

Work 5 (7, 7, 7, 5, 5, 7) rows even. Rep the last 6 (8, 8, 8, 6, 6, 8) rows 1 (4, 4, 4, 3, 2, 2) more time(s), then rep dec row every 8 (0, 0, 0, 8, 8, 10) rows 3 (0, 0, 0, 2, 3, 2) times—31 (34, 37, 40, 43, 46, 51) sts rem.

Work 7 rows even, ending with a WS row.

NOTE: Neck shaping is introduced while waist shaping is in progress and armhole shaping is introduced while neck shaping is in progress; read all the way through the foll sections before proceeding.

INC ROW: (RS) Keeping in patt, work to last st, M1, k1—1 st inc'd.

Work 5 (3, 5, 3, 3, 3, 3) rows even. Rep the last 6 (4, 6, 4, 4, 4, 4) rows 3 (1, 3, 1, 1, 2, 2) more time(s), then rep dec row every 8 (6, 8, 6, 6, 6, 6) rows 2 (5, 2, 5, 5, 4, 4) times.

At the same time when piece measures 11½ (12, 12, 12¼, 12¾, 13, 13¼)" (29 [30.5, 30.5, 31, 32.5, 33, 33.5] cm) from CO, ending with a WS row, shape neck as foll.

Shape Neck

DEC ROW: (RS) Cont waist shaping as established, k1, ssk, work to end—1 st dec'd.

Keeping in patt, work 1 row even. Rep the last 2 rows 1 (3, 0, 4, 4, 3, 2) more time(s), then rep dec row every 4 rows 14 (13, 15, 13, 13, 14, 15) time(s).

At the same time when piece measures 13¾ (14, 14, 14, 14¼, 14¼, 14¼)" (35 [35.5, 35.5, 35.5, 36, 36, 36] cm) from CO, ending with a RS row, shape armhole as foll.

Shape Armhole

With WS facing, BO 5 (6, 6, 6, 7, 7, 8) sts, work to end. Dec 1 st at armhole edge (end of RS rows; beg of WS rows) every row 2 (3, 3, 3, 3, 5, 7) times, then every RS row 0 (0, 2, 4, 4, 4, 4) times. Cont neck shaping, work in patt until armhole measures 7¼ (7½, 7¾, 8, 8¼, 8¾, 9¼)" (18.5 [19, 19.5, 20.5, 21, 22, 23.5] cm), ending with a RS row—14 (15, 16, 16, 18, 19, 21) sts rem after all shaping is completed.

Shape Shoulder

At shoulder edge (beg of WS rows), BO 5 (5, 5, 5, 6, 6, 7) sts 2 times, then BO rem 4 (5, 6, 6, 6, 7, 7) sts.

Sleeves

With MC and smaller needles, CO 42 (46, 46, 50, 50, 54, 58) sts.

SET-UP ROW: (WS) P2, *k2, p2; rep from *.

Work in rib as established until piece measures 3" (7.5 cm) from CO, ending with a WS row. Change to larger needles and St st and work 2 rows even, ending with a WS row.

Shape Sleeve

INC ROW: (RS) K1, M1, work to last st, M1, k1—2 sts inc'd.

Work 13 (15, 13, 13, 11, 11, 7) rows even. Rep the last 14 (16, 14, 14, 12, 12, 8) rows 3 (2, 2, 1, 1, 8, 2) more times(s), then rep inc row every 16 (18, 16, 16, 14, 0, 10) rows 3 (3, 4, 5, 6, 0, 8) times—56 (58, 60, 64, 66, 72, 80) sts. Work even until sleeve measures 18 (18¼, 18¼, 18½, 18¾, 18¾, 18¾)" (45.5 [46.5, 46.5, 47, 47.5, 47.5, 47.5] cm) from CO, ending with a WS row.

Shape Cap

BO 5 (6, 6, 6, 7, 7, 8) sts at beg of next 2 rows—46 (46, 48, 52, 52, 58, 64) sts rem. Dec 1 st each end of needle every RS row 6 (6, 5, 5, 5, 6, 6) times, then every 4 rows 2 (2, 3, 3, 3, 3, 2) times, then every RS row 3 (3, 4, 3, 5, 4, 6) times, then every row 3 (3, 3, 5, 3, 5, 7) times—18 (18, 18, 20, 20, 22, 22) sts rem. BO 3 sts at beg of next 2 rows—12 (12, 12, 14, 14, 16, 16) sts rem. BO all sts.

Finishing

Block pieces to measurements. With yarn threaded on a tapestry needle, sew shoulder seams. Sew sleeves into armholes. Sew sleeve and side seams taking care to align stripes.

Fronts and Neckband

With smaller cir needle, RS facing, and beg at lower right front edge, pick up and knit 65 (67, 67, 68, 70, 72, 73) sts evenly spaced to beg of neck shaping, 50 (50, 50, 52, 52, 53,

54) sts to shoulder seam, 44 (44, 44, 46, 46, 48, 48) sts across back neck to other shoulder seam, 50 (50, 50, 52, 52, 53, 54) sts to base of neck shaping, and 65 (67, 67, 68, 70, 72, 73) sts to lower left front edge—274 (278, 278, 286, 290, 298, 302) sts total.

SET-UP ROW: (WS) P2, *k2, p2; rep from *.

Work in rib as established for 2 more rows, ending with a WS row.

BUTTONHOLE ROW: (RS) Keeping in rib patt, work 5 (4, 4, 5, 6, 5, 6) sts, *sl 1 purlwise with yarn in front (pwise wyf), bring yarn to back [sl 1, pass first slipped st over second slipped st to BO 1 st] 3 times, slip rem st from right needle tip to left needle tip, turn work so WS is facing and use the cable method (see Glossary) to CO 4 sts, turn work so RS is facing, sl the first st on the left needle tip to the right needle tip, then lift the extra CO st over the adjacent st and off the right needle to close the buttonhole, work 10 (11, 11, 11, 12, 12) sts in rib patt; rep from * 4 more times, work to end.

Work 3 rows even in rib, ending with a WS row. With RS facing, BO all sts in patt.

Weave in loose ends. Block again, if desired.

FINISHED SIZE

About 8½" (21.5 cm) hand circumference and 12½" (31.5 cm) long.

Note: For larger mittens, use larger needles for fewer stitches/inch.

YARN

Fingering weight (#1 Super Fine).

Shown here: O-Wool Classic 2-ply (100% certified organic merino; 198 yd [181 m]/50 g): #1000 natural (MC), #4304 evergreen (CC1), #4411 begonia (CC2), and #5203 indigo (CC3), 1 skein each.

NEEDLES

Cuff: size U.S. 1 (2.25 mm): set of 4 or 5 double-pointed (dpn).

Hand: size U.S. 2 (2.5 mm): set of 4 or 5 dpn.

Adjust needle size if necessary to obtain the correct gauge.

NOTIONS

Marker (m); waste yarn or stitch holder; tapestry needle.

GAUGE

28 sts and 36 rnds = 4" (10 cm) in rosebud patt, worked in rnds on larger needles.

DAMASK MITTENS

DESIGNED BY *Kristen Rengren*

These mittens were broadly inspired by a WWII-era cardigan-and-pullover set, originally published in the 1940s in the British crafting magazine *Stitchcraft*. The original twinset paired colorful stripes with a lovely stranded rose motif for a delicate, feminine effect. Scaled down significantly and rendered with only two colors at a time (instead of four, as in the original), the roses are just as sweet and reminiscent of a bygone era, but much easier to knit! They are small enough for a take-along project.

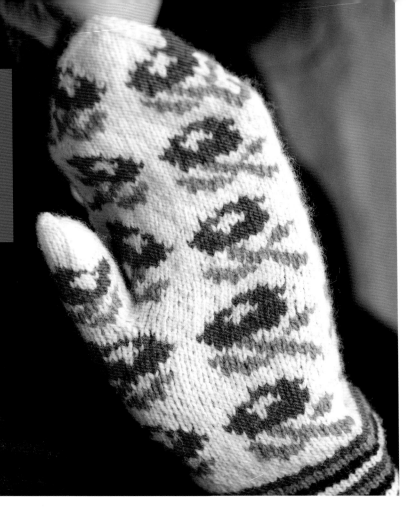

Stitch Guide

Stripe Pattern

RNDS 1 AND 2: With CC1, knit.

RNDS 3 AND 4: With CC2, knit.

RNDS 5 AND 6: With MC, knit.

RNDS 7 AND 8: With CC3, knit.

Rep Rnds 1–8 for patt.

Mitten

With CC3 and smaller needles, CO 60 sts. Place marker (pm) and join for working in rnds, being careful not to twist sts.

Knit 7 rnds.

TURNING RND: *K2tog, yo; rep from *.

Knit 4 rnds even, then work Rnds 1–8 of stripe patt (see Stitch Guide) 2 times, then work Rnds 1–4 once more—piece measures about 3¾" (9.5 cm) from CO.

With MC and larger needles, knit 1 rnd even, then work Rnds 1–14 of Rosebud chart 2 times, then work Rnd 1 again—piece measures about 7¼" (18.5 cm) from CO.

Divide for Thumb

Work the left and right hands as foll.

LEFT HAND ONLY

NEXT RND: Keeping in patt, work Rnd 2 of chart over 18 sts, place next 12 sts on waste yarn or holder for thumb, work to end of rnd.

NEXT RND: Keeping in patt, work Rnd 3 of chart over 18 sts, use MC and the backward-loop method (see Glossary) to CO 12 sts over the gap, work to end of rnd.

□ with MC, knit ⟍ ssk

△ with CC1, knit ⟋ k2tog

− with CC2, knit ▨ no stitch

▢ pattern repeat

ROSEBUD

DECREASE

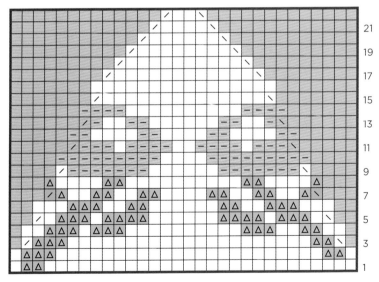

RIGHT HAND ONLY

NEXT RND: Place the first 12 sts on waste yarn or holder for thumb, work Rnd 2 of chart to end of rnd.

NEXT RND: With MC, use the backward-loop method to CO 12 sts over the gap, work Rnd 3 of chart to end of rnd.

BOTH HANDS

Work Rnds 4–14 of chart, then work Rnds 1–14 again. Work Rnds 1–22 of Decrease chart—8 sts rem.

Cut yarn, leaving a 6" (15 cm) tail. Thread tail on a tapestry needle, draw through rem sts, pull tight to close hole, and fasten off on WS.

Thumb

Transfer 12 held thumb sts onto dpn. With RS facing, join MC to end of thumb sts, then pick up and knit 12 sts along CO edge of upper hand—24 sts total. Divide sts evenly on 3 dpn.

Work the left and right hand as foll.

LEFT HAND ONLY

SET-UP ROW: Join for working in rnds, k14, pm for beg of rnd.

Work Rnds 1–28 of Left Thumb chart, working decs as indicated—2 sts rem.

Cut yarn, leaving a 6″ (15 cm) tail. Thread tail on a tapestry needle, draw through rem sts, pull tight to close hole, and fasten off on WS.

RIGHT HAND ONLY

SET-UP ROW: Join for working in rnds, pm for beg of rnd.

Work Rnds 1–28 of Right Thumb chart, working dec as indicated—2 sts rem.

Cut yarn, leaving a 6″ (15 cm) tail. Thread tail on a tapestry needle, draw through rem sts, pull tight to close hole, and fasten off on WS.

Finishing

Fold cuff facing to WS along turning rnd and, with CC3 threaded on a tapestry needle, use a whipstitch (see Glossary) to sew in place, being careful to prevent the hem from biasing.

Weave in loose ends and close any gaps around thumb. Steam-block to measurements.

with MC, knit   ssk

with CC1, knit   k2tog

with CC2, knit   no stitch

LEFT THUMB

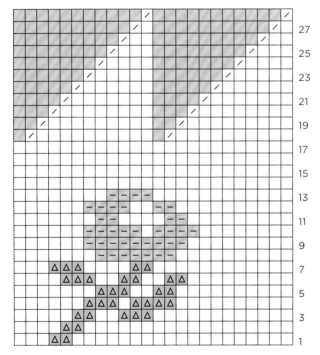

RIGHT THUMB

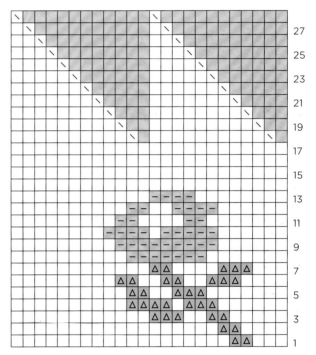

FINISHED SIZE
About 30¼ (34¼, 38¼, 42¼, 46¼, 50¼)" (77 [87, 97, 107.5, 117.5, 127.5] cm) bust circumference, buttoned.

Coat shown measures 34¼" (87 cm).

YARN
Worsted weight (#4 Medium).

Shown here: Rowan Lima (84% baby alpaca, 8% merino, 8% nylon; 109 yd [100 m]/50 g): #888 lima (tan; MC), 12 (13, 14, 16, 18, 19) skeins; #878 Patagonia (navy; CC), 2 (3, 3, 3, 3, 3) skeins.

NEEDLES
Body, hood, and sleeves: size U.S. 8 (5 mm): 24" (60 cm) circular (cir) and set of 4 or 5 double-pointed (dpn).

Lining: size U.S. 7 (4.5 mm): 24" (60 cm) cir and set or 4 or 5 dpn.

Adjust needle size if necessary to obtain the correct gauge.

NOTIONS
Smooth waste yarn of comparable gauge for provisional cast-on; markers (m); stitch holders; tapestry needle; four 1" (2.5 cm) buttons.

GAUGE
18 sts and 26 rows = 4" (10 cm) in St st on larger needles.

COBBLESTONE TRENCHCOAT

DESIGNED BY *Veera Välimäki*

For this sweater coat, I was inspired by a recent visit to Boston. Even though it was nearly winter, the sun was incredibly warm and the streets of nearby Cambridge were full of life. Everyone looked as if they had known each other forever—it felt like magic. With this design, I wanted to capture that visible feeling of warmth and togetherness. The lower body of the coat is worked in one piece to the armholes and then divided for the fronts and back. For the sleeves, stitches are picked up from armhole, the caps are shaped with short-rows, then knitted in the round to the bind-offs at the cuffs.

Body

With CC and smaller cir needle, use a provisional method (see Glossary) to CO 186 (204, 222, 240, 258, 276) sts. Do not join.

Work even in St st (knit RS rows; purl WS rows) until piece measures 3" (7.5 cm) from CO, ending with WS row. Change to MC and knit 1 RS row.

Change to larger cir needle and knit 1 WS row for turning ridge. Cont even in St st until piece measures 3" (7.5 cm) from turning ridge, ending with a WS row.

JOIN HEM: With RS facing, carefully remove waste yarn from provisional CO and place exposed sts on smaller cir needle. Hold the 2 needles parallel with WS of fabric facing tog. *Work the first st on each needle tog as k2tog; rep from *—still 186 (204, 222, 240, 258, 276) sts.

Work even in St st until piece measures 17¾ (17¾, 18, 18¼, 18½, 18½)" (45 [45, 45.5, 46.5, 47, 47] cm) from CO, ending with a WS row.

DEC ROW: (RS) K20 (22, 24, 26, 28, 30), [k4tog, k2] 2 times, k4tog, k39 (46, 53, 60, 67, 74), [ssssk (see Glossary), k2] 2 times, ssssk, k4, [k4tog, k2] 2 times, k4tog, k39 (46, 53, 60, 67, 74), [ssssk, k2] 2 times, ssssk, knit to end—150 (168, 186, 204, 222, 240) sts rem.

Work 1 WS row even.

NOTE: The body is divided for the fronts and back while the buttonholes are in progress. Read all the way through the following section before proceeding.

BUTTONHOLE ROW: (RS) K8, yo, k2tog, knit to end.

[Work even for 3 (3, 3, 3¼, 3½, 3¾)" (7.5 [7.5, 7.5, 8.5, 9, 9.5] cm), ending with a WS row, then rep buttonhole row] 2 times—3 buttonholes.

At the same time when piece measures 21¾ (21¾, 22, 22¼, 22½, 22½)" (55 [55, 56, 56.5, 57, 57] cm) from CO, ending with a WS row, divide for fronts and back as foll.

Divide for Fronts and Back

With RS facing, k39 (43, 47, 51, 54, 58) for right front and place these sts on a holder, k4 (6, 6, 8, 10, 12) for right underarm and place these sts on a separate holder, k64 (70, 80,

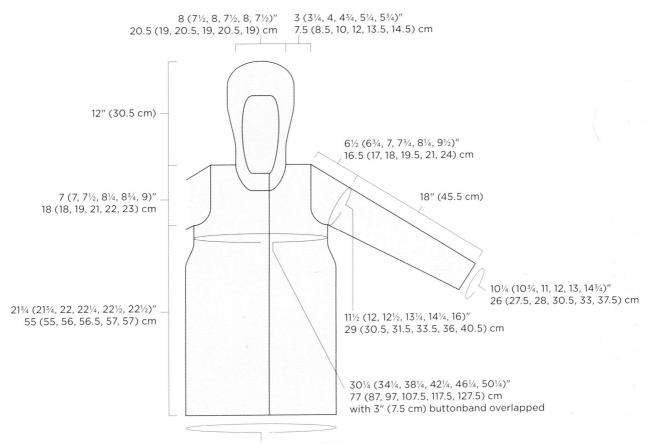

8 (7½, 8, 7½, 8, 7½)"
20.5 (19, 20.5, 19, 20.5, 19) cm

3 (3¼, 4, 4¾, 5¼, 5¾)"
7.5 (8.5, 10, 12, 13.5, 14.5) cm

12" (30.5 cm)

6½ (6¾, 7, 7¾, 8¼, 9½)"
16.5 (17, 18, 19.5, 21, 24) cm

18" (45.5 cm)

7 (7, 7½, 8¼, 8¾, 9)"
18 (18, 19, 21, 22, 23) cm

10¼ (10¾, 11, 12, 13, 14¾)"
26 (27.5, 28, 30.5, 33, 37.5) cm

21¾ (21¾, 22, 22¼, 22½, 22½)"
55 (55, 56, 56.5, 57, 57) cm

11½ (12, 12½, 13¼, 14¼, 16)"
29 (30.5, 31.5, 33.5, 36, 40.5) cm

30¼ (34¼, 38¼, 42¼, 46¼, 50¼)"
77 (87, 97, 107.5, 117.5, 127.5) cm
with 3" (7.5 cm) buttonband overlapped

38¼ (42¼, 46¼, 50¼, 54¼, 58¼)"
97 (107.5, 117.5, 127.5, 138, 148) cm
with 3" (7.5 cm) buttonband overlapped

86, 94, 100) for back and place these sts on a separate holder, k4 (6, 6, 8, 10, 12) for left underarm and place these sts on a separate holder, knit to end for left front—39 (43, 47, 51, 54, 58) sts for each front, 64 (70, 80, 86, 94, 100) for back.

Left Front

Working 39 (43, 47, 51, 54, 58) left front sts, purl 1 WS row.

DEC ROW: (RS) K2, ssk, knit to end—1 st dec'd.

Rep dec row every RS row 0 (2, 3, 4, 4, 6) times—38 (40, 43, 46, 49, 51) sts rem.

Cont even in St st until armhole measures 4 (4, 4½, 5¼, 5¾, 6)″ (10 [10, 11.5, 13.5, 14.5, 15] cm), ending with a RS row.

Shape Neck

With WS facing, p20 and place these sts onto holder for neck, purl to end—18 (20, 23, 26, 29, 31) sts rem.

DEC ROW: (RS) Knit to last 4 sts, k2tog, k2—1 st dec'd.

Rep dec row every RS row 4 more times—13 (15, 18, 21, 24, 26) sts rem. Cont in St st until armhole measures 7 (7, 7½, 8¼, 8¾, 9)″ (18 [18, 19, 21, 22, 23] cm), ending with a WS row.

Cut yarn and place sts on holder.

Right Front

Place 39 (43, 47, 51, 54, 58) right front sts on larger cir needle and rejoin yarn with WS facing. Purl 1 WS row. Working buttonholes as established, cont as foll:

DEC ROW: (RS) Knit to last 4 sts, k2tog, k2—1 st dec'd.

Rep dec row every RS row 0 (2, 3, 4, 4, 6) more times—38 (40, 43, 46, 49, 51) sts rem.

Cont even in St st until armhole measures 4 (4, 4½, 5¼, 5¾, 6)″ (10 [10, 11.5, 13.5, 14.5, 15] cm), ending with a RS row.

Shape Neck

With WS facing, purl to last 20 sts, place rem 20 sts on holder for neck—18 (20, 23, 26, 29, 31) sts rem.

DEC ROW: (RS) K2, ssk, knit to end—1 st dec'd.

Rep dec row every RS row 4 more times—13 (15, 18, 21, 24, 26) sts rem. Cont in St st until armhole measures 7 (7, 7½, 8¼, 8¾, 9)″ (18 [18, 19, 21, 22, 23] cm), ending with a WS row.

Cut yarn and place sts on holder.

Back

Place 64 (70, 80, 86, 94, 100) held back sts on larger cir needle and rejoin yarn with WS facing. Purl 1 WS row.

DEC ROW: (RS) K2, ssk, knit to 4 last sts, k2tog, k2—2 sts dec'd.

Rep dec row every RS row 0 (2, 3, 4, 4, 6) more times—62 (64, 72, 76, 84, 86) sts rem. Cont even in St st until armholes measure 5 (5, 5½, 6¼, 6¾, 7)″ (12.5 [12.5, 14, 16, 17, 18] cm), ending with a WS row.

Shape Neck

With RS facing, k16 (18, 21, 24, 27, 29) for right shoulder, BO 30 (28, 30, 28, 30, 28) for back neck, k16 (18, 21, 24, 27, 29) for left shoulder. Work each shoulder separately as foll.

LEFT SHOULDER
Purl 1 WS row.

DEC ROW: (RS) K2, ssk, knit to end—1 st dec'd.

Rep dec row every RS row 2 more times—13 (15, 18, 21, 24, 26) sts rem. Cont in St st until armhole measures 7 (7, 7½, 8¼, 8¾, 9)″ (18 [18, 19, 21, 22, 23] cm), ending with a WS row.

Cut yarn and place sts on holder.

9)" (18 [18, 19, 21, 22, 23] cm), ending with a WS row.

Cut yarn and place sts on one larger dpn.

Join Shoulders

Place 13 (15, 18, 21, 24, 26) right front shoulder sts on one larger dpn. Holding needles parallel with RS of fabric facing tog, use the three-needle method (see Glossary) to BO right front and back sts tog. Rep for left shoulder.

Hood

With MC, larger cir needle, RS facing, and beg at end of held right front sts (keep right front sts on holder), pick up and knit 22 sts evenly spaced to held back neck sts, pm, k30 (28, 30, 28, 30, 28) held back neck sts, pm, pick up and knit 22 sts evenly spaced to beg of held left front sts (keep left front sts on holder)—74 (72, 74, 72, 74, 72) sts total.

Work even in St st for 2" (5 cm), ending with a WS row.

Shape Hood

INC ROW: (RS) *Knit to 2 sts before m, M1R (see Glossary), k2, slip marker (sl m), k2, M1L (see Glossary); rep from * once, knit to end—4 sts inc'd.

Work 3 rows even. Rep the last 4 rows 5 more times—98 (96, 98, 96, 98, 96) sts. Cont in St st until hood measures 12" (30.5 cm) from pick-up row, ending with a WS row.

Work short-rows as foll:

With RS facing, knit to second m, remove m, ssk, turn work so WS is facing, purl to

RIGHT SHOULDER

With WS facing, rejoin yarn to 16 (18, 21, 24, 27, 29) right shoulder sts. Work 1 WS row even.

DEC ROW: (RS) Knit to 4 last sts, k2tog, k2—1 st dec'd.

Rep dec row every RS row 2 more times—13 (15, 18, 21, 24, 26) sts rem. Cont in St st until until armhole measures 7 (7, 7½, 8¼, 8¾,

Cobblestone Trenchcoat

previous m, remove m, p2tog, turn work so RS is facing. *Knit to previous ssk, ssk (previous ssk plus next st), turn work so WS is facing, purl to previous p2tog, p2tog (previous p2tog plus next st), turn work to RS is facing; rep from * until all outer sts are decreased—44 (42, 44, 42, 44, 42) sts rem.

Cut yarn and place sts on smaller cir needle.

Edging

Place 20 held right front neck sts on larger cir needle and join MC with WS facing. With WS facing, p20 right front sts.

With RS facing, k20, pick up and knit 44 sts evenly spaced along right edge of hood, k44 (42, 44, 42, 44, 42) held hood sts, pick up and knit 44 sts along left edge of hood, k20 held left front sts—172 (170, 172, 170, 172, 170) sts total.

Work even in St st for 1½" (3.8 cm). Work buttonhole as before, then work even in St st until edging measures 3" (7.5 cm) from pick-up row, ending with a RS row. Knit 1 WS row for turning ridge. Change to smaller needle and knit 1 RS row. Change to CC and work even in St st for 3" (7.5 cm), working another buttonhole after 1½" (3.8 cm). BO all sts.

Sleeves

With RS facing, place the first 2 (3, 3, 4, 5, 6) held underarm sts on one larger dpn, then place rem 2 (3, 3, 4, 5, 6) held sts on another larger dpn.

With RS facing, join MC and, beg at center of held underarm sts with another larger dpn, k2 (3, 3, 4, 5, 6) sts, then pick up and knit 24 (24, 25, 26, 27, 30) sts evenly spaced to shoulder seam, pm, pick up and knit 24 (24,

25, 26, 27, 30) sts evenly spaced to beg of rem underarm sts, k2 (3, 3, 4, 5, 6)—52 (54, 56, 60, 64, 72) sts total.

Shape Cap

Work short-rows as foll:

SET-UP ROW: With RS facing, knit to 6 sts past shoulder marker, turn work so WS is facing, yo, purl to 6 sts past shoulder marker, turn work.

SHORT-ROW 1: With RS facing, yo, knit to previous yo, k2tog (the previous yo with the next st), turn work.

SHORT-ROW 2: With WS facing, yo, purl to previous yo, ssp (see Glossary; the yo with the next st), turn work.

Rep Short-Rows 1 and 2, working 1 st past the previous yo each row, until you reach the underarm sts, ending with a WS row. Knit to end of rnd. Cont by working all sts in the rnd, with RS facing.

Work even in St st for 2" (5 cm).

DEC RND: K2tog, knit to last 2 sts, ssk—2 sts dec'd.

Work 19 rnds even. Rep dec rnd. Rep the last 20 rnds 1 time—46 (48, 50, 54, 58, 66) sts rem.

Work even until sleeve measures 18" (45.5 cm) from pick-up rnd or desired total length. Purl 1 rnd for turning ridge.

Change to CC and smaller dpn. Work even in St st until facing measures 2" (5 cm) from turning ridge. Loosely BO all sts. Cut yarn, leaving a 24" (61 cm) tail.

Fold facing to WS along turning ridge and, with CC tail threaded on a tapestry needle, sew BO edge to WS of sleeve.

Pockets (make 2)

With MC and larger cir needle CO 30 sts. Do not join. Knit 1 RS row. Work short-rows as foll:

SET-UP ROW: With WS facing, purl to last 7 sts, turn work so RS is facing, yo, knit to last 7 sts, turn work.

SHORT-ROW 1: With WS facing yo, purl to previous yo, ssp (the previous yo with next st), turn work.

SHORT-ROW 2: With RS facing, yo, knit to previous yo, k2tog (the yo with next st), turn work.

Rep Short-Rows 1 and 2, working 1 st past the previous yo each row, until 3 sts rem after each yo.

NEXT ROW: (WS) Yo, purl to previous yo, ssp (the yo with next st), purl to end.

NEXT ROW: (RS) Knit to previous yo, k2tog (the yo with next st), knit to end.

Cont even in St st until pocket measures 6" (15 cm) from CO, ending with a WS row. Purl 1 RS row for turning ridge. Purl 1 WS row. Change to smaller cir needle and knit 1 row. Change to CC and cont in St st until facing measures 2" (5 cm) from turning ridge. BO all sts leaving a 12" (30.5 cm) tail.

Finishing

Fold hood facing to WS along turning ridge and, with CC threaded on a tapestry needle, sew BO edge to WS of hood.

Fold facing to WS along turning ridge and, with CC threaded on a tapestry, sew BO edge to WS of pocket.

With MC threaded on a tapestry needle, sew pockets to fronts, positioning them 4" (10 cm) away from center front and 4" (10 cm) up from hem.

With MC, sew buttons to left front, opposite buttonholes.

Weave in loose ends. Block to measurements.

FINISHED SIZE

Hat: About 21" (53.5 cm) head circumference and 8½" (21.5 cm) tall.

Mittens: About 8" (20.5 cm) hand circumference and 9½" (24 cm) hand length.

YARN

Worsted weight (#4 Medium).

Shown here: The Fibre Company Organik (70% organic merino, 15% baby alpaca, 15% silk; 98 yd [89 m]/50 g): seawater (MC), 2 skeins; Oahu (CC1), lichen (CC2), arctic tundra (CC3), and atoll (CC4), 1 skein each.

NEEDLES

Hat ribbing: size U.S. 4 (3.5 mm): 16" (40 cm) circular (cir).

Hat body: size U.S. 6 (4 mm): 16" (40 cm) cir and set of 4 or 5 double-pointed (dpn).

Mitten ribbing: size U.S. 4 (3.5 mm): set of 4 or 5 double-pointed (dpn).

Mitten hand: size U.S. 6 (4 mm): set of 4 or 5 dpn.

Adjust needle size if necessary to obtain the correct gauge.

NOTIONS

Markers (m); tapestry needle.

GAUGE

22 sts and 24 rnds = 4" (10 cm) in charted patt on larger needles, worked in rnds.

MORRIS COVE HAT & MITTENS

DESIGNED BY *Kate Gagnon Osborn*

With fall comes the end of sticky, humid summer days and the need for warm woolly accessories to protect exposed heads, hands, and necks. This hat-and-mittens set, with nautical-inspired colors and Fair Isle patterning (that provides an extra layer of warmth) is the perfect anecdote to unpredictable temperatures. The use of only two colors per round makes either project ideal for first-time colorwork. The jogless stripes at the top of the hat, mittens, and thumbs finish off the set with ease.

Hat

With MC and smaller cir needle, CO 96 sts. Place marker (pm) and join for working in rnds, being careful not to twist sts.

SET-UP RND: *K2, p2; rep from *.

Work in rib as established until piece measures 1½" (3.8 cm) from CO.

INC RND: K1, *M1 (see Glossary), k6; rep from * to last 5 sts, M1, k5—112 sts.

Change to larger cir needle.

Work Rnds 1–25 of Fair Isle A chart, then work Rnds 1–4 of Fair Isle B chart—96 sts rem; piece measures about 6¼" (16 cm) from CO.

Decrease for Crown

RND 1: With CC3, knit.

RND 2: With CC3, remove m, sl 1 purlwise with yarn in back (pwise wyb), replace m, knit to end.

RND 3: With MC, knit.

RND 4: With MC, remove m, sl 1 pwise wyb, replace m, k1, k2tog, *k4, k2tog; rep from * to last 3 sts, k3—80 sts rem.

RND 5: With CC3, knit.

RND 6: With CC3, remove m, sl 2 pwise wyb, replace m, *k3, k2tog; rep from *—64 sts rem.

RND 7: With MC, knit.

RND 8: With MC, remove m, sl 1 pwise wyb, replace m, k1, k2tog, *k2, k2tog; rep from to last st, k1*—48 sts rem.

RND 9: With CC3, knit.

RND 10: With CC3, remove m, sl 2 pwise wyb, replace m, *k1, k2tog; rep from *—32 sts rem.

RND 11: With MC, knit.

RND 12: With MC, remove m, sl 2 pwise wyb, replace m, *k2tog; rep from *—16 sts rem.

RND 13: With CC3, knit.

RND 14: With CC3, *k2tog; rep from *—8 sts rem.

Legend:

- ◢ (with MC, knit)
- △ (with CC1, knit)
- • (with CC2, knit)
- ☐ (with CC3, knit)
- ⊙ (with CC4, knit)
- ╱ (k2tog in indicated color)

FAIR ISLE A

(chart with rows numbered 1, 3, 5, 7, 9, 11, 13, 15, 17, 19, 21, 23, 25)

FAIR ISLE B

(chart with rows numbered 1, 3)

Finishing

Cut yarn, leaving a 6" (15 cm) tail. Draw tail through rem sts, pull tight to close top, and fasten off on WS.

Weave in loose ends. Block lightly.

Mittens

With MC and smaller dpn, CO 40 sts. Arrange sts on 3 or 4 dpn, place marker (pm), and join for working in rnds, being careful not to twist sts.

SET-UP RND: *K2, p2; rep from *.

Work in rib as established until piece measures 1½" (3.8 cm) from CO.

INC RND: K5, M1 (see Glossary), *k10, M1; rep from * to last 5 sts, k5—44 sts.

Work right and left hands as foll:

RIGHT HAND
Work Rnds 1–8 of Right Hand chart 2 times, then work Rnds 1–7 once more—piece measures about 5¼" (13.5 cm) from CO.

NEXT RND: (Mark thumb) With MC, k4, k7 with waste yarn, return 7 sts just worked onto left needle tip, knit them again with MC, then knit to end.

Work Rnds 1–8 of Right Hand chart 2 times, then work Rnds 1–4 once more—piece measures about 8¾" (22 cm) from CO.

LEFT HAND

Work Rnds 1–8 of Left Hand chart 2 times, then work Rnds 1–7 once more—piece measures about 5¼" (13.5 cm) from CO.

NEXT RND: (Mark thumb) With MC, k33, k7 with waste yarn, return 7 sts just worked onto left needle tip, knit them again with MC, then knit to end.

Work Rnds 1–8 of Left Hand chart 2 times, then work Rnds 1–4 once more—piece measures about 8¾" (22 cm) from CO.

Shape Top

RND 1: With CC3, knit.

RND 2: With CC3, remove m, sl 1 purlwise with yarn in back (pwise wyb), replace m, *k2tog, k16, ssk, k2; rep from *—40 sts rem.

RND 3: With MC, knit.

RND 4: With MC, remove m, sl 2 pwise wyb, replace m, *k14, ssk, k2, k2tog; rep from *—36 sts rem.

RND 5: With CC3, knit.

RND 6: With CC3, remove m, sl 1 pwise wyb, replace m, *k12, ssk, k2, k2tog; rep from *—32 sts rem.

RND 7: With MC, knit.

RND 8: With MC, remove m, sl 1 pwise wyb, replace m, *k10, ssk, k2, k2tog; rep from *—28 sts rem.

RND 9: With CC3, knit.

RND 10: With CC3, remove m, sl 1, replace m, *k8, ssk, k2, k2tog; rep from *—24 sts rem.

RND 11: With MC, knit.

RND 12: With MC, remove m, sl 1 pwise wyb, replace m, *k6, ssk, k2, k2tog; rep from *—20 sts rem.

RND 13: With CC3, knit.

RND 14: With CC3, remove m, sl 1 pwise wyb, replace m, *k4, ssk, k2, k2tog; rep from *—16 sts rem.

	with MC, knit
	with CC1, knit
	with CC2, knit
	with CC3, knit
	with CC4, knit

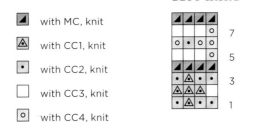

LEFT HAND

RIGHT HAND

With CC3, k6, cut yarn, leaving a 10″ (25.5 cm) tail. Divide sts so that there are 8 palm sts on one dpn and 8 back-of-hand sts on a second dpn. Thread tail on a tapestry needle and use the Kitchener st (see Glossary) to graft sts tog.

Thumb

Remove waste yarn from held sts and place 6 exposed top sts and 7 exposed bottom sts on separate dpns. With MC, pick up and knit 2 st in space between upper and lower set of sts, k7 lower sts, pick up and knit 1 sts in space between lower and upper sts, then pm for beg of rnd—16 sts total.

Work jogless stripes as foll:

RND 1: With CC3, knit.

RND 2: With CC3, remove m, sl 1 pwise wyb, replace m, knit to end.

RND 3: With MC, knit.

RND 4: With MC, remove m, sl 1, replace m, knit to end.

Rep Rnds 1–4 two more times.

SHAPE TOP

RND 1: With CC3, knit.

RND 2: With CC3, remove m, sl 1 pwise wyb, replace m, *k2tog, k2; rep from * to end—12 sts rem.

RND 3: With MC, knit.

RND 4: With MC, remove m, sl 1 pwise wyb, replace m, *k2tog, k1; rep from * to end—8 sts rem.

RND 5: With CC3, knit.

RND 6: With CC3, *k2tog; rep from *— 4 sts rem.

Finishing

Cut yarn, leaving a 6″ (15 cm) tail. Draw tail through rem sts, pull tight to close top, and fasten off on WS.

Weave in loose ends. Block to measurements.

FINISHED SIZE

About 31¼ (35½, 39½, 43¾, 47¾, 52)" (79.5 [90, 100.5, 111, 121.5, 132] cm) bust circumference, buttoned.

Sweater shown measures 35½" (90 cm).

Note: This garment is designed for a close fit with zero ease.

YARN

Fingering weight (#1 Super Fine).

Shown here: Jamieson's Shetland Spindrift (100% Shetland wool; 115 yd [105 m]/ 25 .g): #150 Atlantic (MC), 8 (9, 10, 11, 12, 13) balls; #1010 seabright (CC1), #259 leprechaun (CC2), #390 daffodil (CC4), and #271 flame (CC5), 1 ball each; #127 ecology pebble (CC3) 1 (1, 1, 2, 2, 2) ball(s).

NEEDLES

Body and sleeves: size U.S. 4 (3.5 mm): 16" (40 cm), 24" (60 cm), and 32" (80 cm) circular (cir) and set of 4 or 5 double-pointed (dpn).

Buttonbands: size U.S. 3 (3.25 mm): 24" (60 cm) cir.

Adjust needle size if necessary to obtain the correct gauge.

NOTIONS

Markers (m); waste yarn; tapestry needle; ten ½" (1.3 cm) buttons.

GAUGE

27 sts and 40 rnds = 4" (10 cm) in St st on larger needles, worked in rnds.

TREFOIL CARDIGAN

DESIGNED BY *Gudrun Johnston*

Trefoil is an updated version of the familiar yoked sweater of the 1970s. This design has waist shaping and a lower neckline creating a more feminine and modern look. The addition of pockets allows casual practicality; the contrast lining adds an unexpected pop of color. The Fair Isle patterning at the yoke is a subtler rendition of the typically large (and often garish) motifs of the past. As this is knitted in 100% Shetland wool, steeks are easily incorporated that allow the body to be worked in the round, then cut without fear of raveling. This cardigan is perfect to throw over a T-shirt and jeans on a crisp fall day!

❖ This cardigan is worked in the round from the bottom up with a steeked center front opening. When cutting steeks, make sure to cut through the exact center of the garment. The center steek sts are included in the total stitch counts given throughout pattern. There are also steeked pocket openings worked in the lower body in the main color only. The pocket steeks are not included in the stitch counts.

❖ At the Fair Isle yoke section, the steek stitches are worked in a vertical stripe pattern as shown in the charts.

❖ When working the charts, read all rounds from right to left and begin and end inside the steek stitches.

Body

With MC and larger, longest cir needle, CO 216 (244, 272, 300 328, 356) sts. Place marker (pm) and join for working in rnds, being careful not to twist sts. The first 3 sts and the last 3 sts are steek sts.

SET UP RIB: K3 (steek sts), *k2 through back loops (tbl), p2; rep from * to last 5 sts, k2tbl, k3 (steek sts).

Cont in twisted rib as established until piece measures 1¾" (4.5 cm) from CO.

NEXT RND: Keeping in patt, work 54 (61, 68, 75, 82, 89) sts for right front, pm for side "seam," work 108 (122, 136, 150, 164, 178) sts for back, pm for other side "seam," work to end for left front.

DEC RND: Keeping in rib patt and working decs as k2tog or p2tog as necessary to maintain patt, dec 2 sts evenly spaced before the first seam m for right front, dec 4 sts evenly spaced before the next seam m for back, and dec 2 sts evenly spaced before the end-of-rnd m for left front—8 sts dec'd; 208 (236, 264, 292, 320, 348) sts rem.

POCKET PLACEMENT RND: K39 (46, 53, 60, 67, 74), pm, use the backward-loop method (see Glossary) to CO 6 sts for right front pocket steek, knit to second side marker, sl m, k13, use the backward-loop method to CO 6 sts for left pocket steek, pm, knit to end.

Knit 7 rnds even.

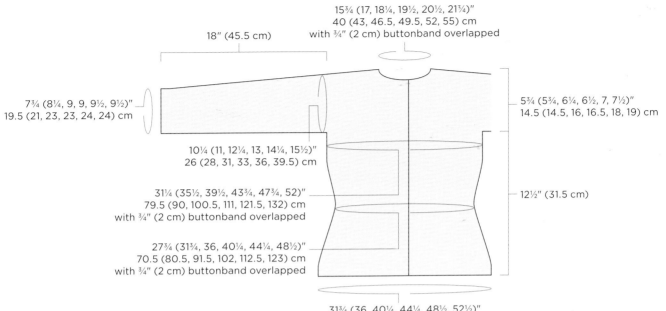

18″ (45.5 cm)

15¾ (17, 18¼, 19½, 20½, 21¾)″
40 (43, 46.5, 49.5, 52, 55) cm
with ¾″ (2 cm) buttonband overlapped

7¾ (8¼, 9, 9, 9½, 9½)″
19.5 (21, 23, 23, 24, 24) cm

5¾ (5¾, 6¼, 6½, 7, 7½)″
14.5 (14.5, 16, 16.5, 18, 19) cm

10¼ (11, 12¼, 13, 14¼, 15½)″
26 (28, 31, 33, 36, 39.5) cm

31¼ (35½, 39½, 43¾, 47¾, 52)″
79.5 (90, 100.5, 111, 121.5, 132) cm
with ¾″ (2 cm) buttonband overlapped

12½″ (31.5 cm)

27¾ (31¾, 36, 40¼, 44¼, 48½)″
70.5 (80.5, 91.5, 102, 112.5, 123) cm
with ¾″ (2 cm) buttonband overlapped

31¾ (36, 40¼, 44¼, 48½, 52½)″
80.5 (91.5, 102, 112.5, 123, 133.5) cm
with ¾″ (2 cm) buttonband overlapped

DEC RND: *Knit to 3 sts before side "seam" m, ssk, k1, slip marker (sl m), k1, k2tog; rep from * once more, knit to end—4 sts dec'd.

Knit 7 rnds even. Rep the last 8 rnds 1 time—200 (228, 256, 284, 312, 340) sts rem, not counting the 12 pocket steek sts.

Rep dec rnd, then work 5 rnds even. Rep the last 6 rnds 2 times—188 (216, 244, 272, 300, 328) sts rem, not counting the 12 pocket steek sts.

Knit 7 rnds even.

NEXT RND: Knit to right pocket m, remove m, BO 6 sts for right pocket steek, knit to 4 sts before left pocket m, BO 6 steek sts removing m, knit to end.

NOTE: A small gap will form next to each set of BO sts on the next rnd, but it will be closed when the pockets are worked.

INC RND: *Knit to 1 st before side "seam" m, M1R (see Glossary), k1, sl m, k1, M1L (see Glossary); rep from * once more, knit to end—4 sts inc'd.

Knit 7 rnds even. Rep the last 8 rnds 1 time—196 (224, 252, 280, 308, 336) sts.

Rep inc rnd, then work 9 rnds even. Rep the last 10 rnds 3 times—212 (240, 268, 296, 324, 352) sts; piece measures about 12½" (31.5 cm) from CO.

Set aside. Do not cut yarn.

Sleeves *(make 2)*

With MC and dpn, CO 52 (56, 60, 64, 68, 72) sts. Divide sts evenly over 3 or 4 needles, pm, and join for working in rnds, being careful not to twist sts.

SET UP RIB: *K2tbl, p2; rep from *.

Work in rib as established until piece measures 3½" (9 cm) from CO.

Knit 1 rnd.

INC RND: K1, M1L, knit to 1 st before m, M1R, k1—2 sts inc'd.

Cont in St st (knit every rnd) and rep inc rnd every 16th (16th, 14th, 14th, 12th, 10th) rnd 3 (3, 3, 1, 2, 4) more time(s), then every 14th (14th, 12th, 12th, 10th, 8th) rnd 3 (3, 5, 4, 4, 8) times, then every 12th (12th, 10th, 10th, 8th, 6th) rnd 2 (2, 2, 6, 7, 3) times—70 (74, 82, 88, 96, 104) sts.

Cont in St st until sleeve measures 18" (45.5 cm) from CO.

Cut yarn. Place first 8 (9, 10, 10, 11, 12) sts and last 8 (9, 10, 10, 11, 12) sts on waste yarn for underarm. Place rem 54 (56, 62, 68, 74, 80) sts on another piece of waste yarn for the yoke.

CHART A

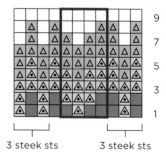

■	with MC, knit
▲	with CC1, knit
△	with CC2, knit
☐	with CC3, knit
☐	pattern repeat

3 steek sts   3 steek sts

Yoke

Return to body with MC still attached. With larger, longest cir needle, and RS facing, knit to 8 (9, 10, 10, 11, 12) sts before side "seam" m, place next 16 (18, 20, 20, 22, 24) sts on waste yarn for underarm, k54 (56, 62, 68, 74, 80) held sleeve sts, knit across sts of back to 8 (9, 10, 10, 11, 12) sts before next side "seam" m, place next 16 (18, 20, 20, 22, 24) sts on waste yarn for other underarm, k54 (56, 62, 68, 74, 80) held sleeve sts, knit to end—288 (316, 352, 392, 428, 464) sts total.

Work even in St st for 5 (5, 9, 13, 17, 21) rnds.

DEC RND 1: K1 (1, 1, 1, 15, 14), k19 (16, 12, 10, 9, 10), k2tog, *k18 (15, 11, 9, 8, 9), k2tog, k19 (16, 12, 10, 9, 10), k2tog; rep from * to last 20 (17, 13, 11, 24, 24) sts, k20 (17, 13, 11, 24, 24)—275 (299, 327, 359, 391, 427) sts rem.

Work Rnds 1–9 of Chart A.

Changing to shorter cir needles when there are too few sts to fit comfortably, dec for your size as foll:

SIZES 31¼ (39½)" ONLY
DEC RND 2: With CC3, k4 (7), *k7 (4), k2tog, k8 (5), k2tog; rep from * to last 5 (8) sts, k5 (8)—247 (279) sts rem.

SIZES 35½ (43¾, 47¾, 52)" ONLY
DEC RND 2: With CC3, k5 (11, 3, 5), *k6 (5, 6, 6), k2tog; rep from * to last 6 (12, 4, 6) sts, k6 (12, 4, 6)—263 (311, 343, 375) sts rem.

ALL SIZES
Knit 3 rnds in CC3, then work Rnds 1–13 of Chart B (see page 99), then knit 3 more rnds in CC3.

Cont for your size as foll:

SIZES 31¼ (35½, 39½)" ONLY
DEC RND 3: With CC3, k3 (3, 11) *k2, k2tog; rep from * to last 4 (4, 12) sts, k4 (4, 12)—187 (199, 215) sts rem.

SIZE 43¾" ONLY
DEC RND 3: With CC3, k8, *k2, k2tog, k1, k2tog; rep from * to last 9 sts, k9—227 sts rem.

SIZES 47¾ (52)" ONLY
DEC RND 3: With CC3, k5 (3), *[k1, k2tog] 2 (4) times, k2, k2tog; rep from * to last 8 (36) sts, [k1, k2tog] 1 (11) times, k5 (3)—243 (259) sts rem.

ALL SIZES
Knit 1 rnd even in CC3, then work Rnds 1–9 of Chart C.

DEC RND 4: With MC, k5, *k2, k2tog; rep from * to last 6 sts, k6—143 (152, 164, 173, 185, 197) sts rem.

Knit 2 rnds in MC and *at the same time* for sizes 31¼ (39½, 43¾, 47¾, 52)", dec 1 st by working (k4, k2tog) once at the beg of the first rnd—142 (152, 163, 172, 184, 196) sts rem.

Work short-rows (see Glossary) in MC to shape neck as foll:

SHORT-ROW 1: (RS) K111 (121, 132, 141, 151, 161) wrap next st, turn work.

SHORT-ROW 2: (WS) P80 (90, 101, 110, 118, 126) wrap next st, turn work.

SHORT-ROWS 3 AND 4: Work in St st (knit RS rows; purl WS rows) to 6 sts before the previous wrapped st, wrap next st, turn work.

NEXT ROW: Knit to end of rnd, working wraps tog with wrapped sts as you come to them.

NEXT RND: Knit 1 rnd, working rem wraps tog with wrapped sts.

DEC RND 5: K3 (4, 4, 6, 4, 1), *k2, k2tog; rep from * to last 3 (4, 3, 6, 4, 3) sts, k3 (4, 3, 6, 4, 3)—108 (116, 124, 132, 140, 148) sts rem.

Neckband

NEXT RND: K3, *k2tbl, p2; rep from * to last 5 sts, k2tbl, k3.

Rep this rnd 4 more times.

BO all sts in patt.

Finishing

Steek

Carefully cut and secure center front steek as described in the Glossary.

Buttonband

NOTE: When picking up sts for the front bands, be sure to pick up between the end of the steek sts and the beg of the body sts.

With MC, smaller cir needle, and RS facing, pick up and knit 130 (130, 134, 138, 142, 146) sts evenly spaced along left front edge. Do not join.

ROW 1: (WS) *P2tbl, k2; rep from * to last 2 sts, p2tbl.

ROW 2: (RS) *K2tbl, p2; rep from * to last 2 sts, k2tbl.

Rep Rows 1 and 2 two more times, then rep Row 1 once more.

BO all sts in rib.

Buttonhole Band

Mark placement of 10 buttonholes on right front edge, one ¾" (2 cm) down from neck edge, one 1" (2.5 cm) up from lower edge, and the others evenly spaced in between.

With MC, smaller cir needle, and RS facing, pick up and knit 130 (130, 134, 138, 142, 146) sts evenly spaced along right front edge. Do not join.

ROWS 1 AND 3: (WS) *P2tbl, k2; rep from * to last 2 sts, p2tbl.

ROW 2: (RS) *K2tbl, p2; rep from * to last 2 sts, k2tbl.

- ⬛ with MC, knit
- ◮ with CC1, knit
- ◭ with CC2, knit
- ☐ with CC3, knit
- Ⅰ with CC4, knit
- ⹀ with CC5, knit
- ◻ pattern repeat

CHART B

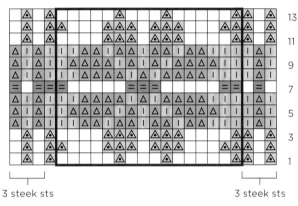

13
11
9
7
5
3
1

3 steek sts   3 steek sts

CHART C

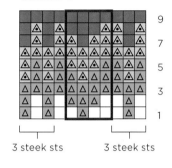

9
7
5
3
1

3 steek sts   3 steek sts

ROW 4: Rep Row 2, but make 3-st 1-row buttonholes (see Glossary) at each buttonhole marker.

Rep Rows 1 and 2 once, then rep Row 1 once more.

BO all sts in rib.

Pockets

Carefully cut and secure pocket steek sts as for center front.

With CC2, smaller cir needle, and RS facing, pick up and knit 33 sts along edge of pocket that is closest to waist and inside the steek sts. Do not join. Beg with a WS row, work even in St st until piece measures 5″ (12.5 cm) from pick-up row.

BO off all sts. Push pocket to WS of work and, with MC threaded on a tapestry needle, sew in place to WS of body.

With MC, smaller cir needle, and RS facing, pick up and knit 33 sts along other edge of pocket. Do not join. With WS facing, BO all sts.

With yarn threaded on a tapestry needle, close any holes at top or bottom of pockets.

Rep for second pocket.

With yarn threaded on a tapestry needle, use the Kitchener st (see Glossary) to graft the held underarm sts tog.

Weave in loose ends. Block to measurements.

Sew buttons to buttonband opposite buttonholes. With MC threaded on a tapestry needle, use a whipstitch (see Glossary) to tack steek sts to WS.

FINISHED SIZE

About 25¼" (64 cm) circumference and 10" (25.5 cm) long.

YARN

Worsted weight (#4 Medium).

Shown here: The Fibre Company Canopy Worsted (50% baby alpaca, 30% merino, 20% viscose from Bamboo; 100 yd [91 m]/50 g): fern (MC); orchid (CC1); quetzal (CC2); 2 skeins each.

NEEDLES

Solid-color sections: size U.S. 4 (3.5 mm): 24" (60 cm) circular (cir).

Stripes and charted sections: size U.S. 5 (3.75 mm): 24" (60 cm) cir.

Adjust needle size if necessary to obtain the correct gauge.

NOTIONS

Marker (m); tapestry needle; smooth waste yarn of comparable gauge for provisional cast-on.

GAUGE

21 sts and 24 rnds = 4" (10 cm) in Fair Isle patt on larger needles, worked in rnds.

21 sts and 30 rnds = 4" (10 cm) in St st on larger needles, worked in rnds.

HILTOn FIELD COWL

DESIGNED BY *Kate Gagnon Osborn*

A combination of stripes and herringbone plaid impart decidedly "ivy league" style to this warm and reversible cowl. Beginning with a provisional cast-on, the piece is worked seamlessly in the round and then the ends are grafted together to create a continuous tube of fabric. Its small size is perfect for throwing in your bag; the double layer of warmth created by the fabric guarantees protection from whatever the weather brings. A bit preppy to provide some fanciful humor to your fall wardrobe, this cowl is both practical in its softness and warmth and stylish in its design.

Stitch Guide

Jogless Stripes

RND 1: With CC1, knit.

RND 2: With CC1, remove m, sl 1 purlwise with yarn in back (pwise wyb), replace m, knit to end.

RND 3: With CC1, knit.

RND 4: With CC2, knit.

RND 5: With CC2, remove m, sl 1 pwise wyb, replace m, knit to end.

RND 6: With CC2, knit.

RND 7: With MC, knit.

RND 8: With MC, remove m, sl 1 pwise wyb, replace m, knit to end.

RND 9: With MC, knit.

Rep Rnds 1–9 for patt.

Cowl

With MC, smaller needle, and using a provisional method (see Glossary) CO 126 sts. Place marker (pm) and join for working in rnds, being careful not to twist sts.

Knit 4 rnds, purl 1 rnd, knit 7 rnds.

INC RND: *K21, M1 (see Glossary); rep from *—132 sts.

Change to larger needle.

Work Rnds 1–9 of jogless stripes (see Stitch Guide) 6 times, then work Rnds 1–6 again.

Change to smaller needle and MC.

Knit 1 rnd.

DEC RND: *K20, k2tog; rep from *—126 sts rem.

Knit 5 rnds, purl 1 rnd, knit 7 rnds.

HERRINGBONE

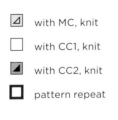

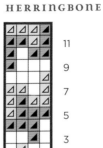

�		

◸ with MC, knit

☐ with CC1, knit

◤ with CC2, knit

☐ pattern repeat

INC RND: *K21, M1; rep from *—132 sts.

Change to larger needle.

Work Rnds 1–12 of Herringbone chart 4 times.

Change to smaller needle and MC.

Knit 1 rnd.

DEC RND: *K20, k2tog; rep from *— 126 sts rem.

Finishing

Weave in loose ends.

Carefully remove waste yarn from provisional CO and place exposed sts on spare cir needle. Fold cowl in half so that WS of stripes are facing WS of herringbone patt to create a tube. With MC threaded on a tapestry needle, use the Kitchener st (see Glossary) to graft sts tog.

Adjust cowl so that purl ridges are at top and bottom, then steam-block to measurements.

SOUTHERN COMFORT

There is something so beautiful, so timeless, about fall in the southern states. Hot, muggy days evolve into cool and breezy afternoons and evenings that are ideal for wearing layered garments. The designs in this collection speak of classic hospitality with an air of sophistication—imagine the smell of warm biscuits, homemade jam, and the comfort of family and friends. These garments and accessories are inspired by evenings devoted to catching up, taking time, slowing down, and enjoying each other's company. The color palette—vintage-inspired hues in soft shades—adds an air of femininity to the overall look and feel of the pieces. A sweet fitted cardigan in an angora blend (complete with a subtle crocheted embellishment at the yoke), a beautiful beaded lace scarf in a gorgeous hand-dyed silk-blend yarn, and a pair of feminine lace leg warmers are just a few of the pieces you'll find within this chapter.

FINISHED SIZE
About 31¼ (33¼, 35¼, 37¼, 39¼, 41¼)" (79.5 [84.5, 89.5, 94.5, 99.5, 105] cm) bust circumference, buttoned with ¾" (2 cm) overlap.

Cardigan shown measures 33¼" (84.5 cm) modeled with 1" (2.5 cm) of negative ease.

YARN
Sportweight (#2 Fine).

Shown here: Classic Elite Yarns Fresco (60% wool, 30% baby alpaca, 10% angora; 164 yd [150 m]/50 g): #5304 sugar blue, 6 (7, 7, 8, 8, 8) skeins.

NEEDLES
Size 5 (3.75 mm): 32" (80 cm) circular (cir) and set of 4 or 5 double-pointed (dpn).

Adjust needle size if necessary to obtain the correct gauge.

NOTIONS
4 stitch markers (m); waste yarn; tapestry needle; 1 removable stitch marker; size E/4 (3.5 mm) crochet hook; eight ½" (3.8 cm) buttons.

GAUGE
24 sts and 32 rows = 4" (10 cm) in St st.

SAVANNAH CARDIGAN

DESIGNED BY *Jane Richmond*

An elegant and understated sweater, this cardigan is designed to be a wardrobe classic. The mixture of fine wool, baby alpaca, and angora creates an incredibly soft garment that can be worn over the barest camisole. The slightly looser-than-recommended gauge ensures a breathable, comfortable fabric with a lighter and more elastic feel. I designed this cardigan to be soft and feminine and to run the gamut from formal to casual, depending on what it is paired with. The hint of vintage is sure to appeal to modern women.

NOTE

❖ Buttonholes are made by beginning wrong-side rows with (k2, yo, k2tog). For even placement, make buttonholes on every 11th garter ridge (every 22 rows), as viewed from the right side.

Yoke

With circular needle CO 56 (56, 56, 62, 62, 62) sts.

SET-UP ROW: (RS) K1 for left front, pm, k10 (10, 10, 12, 12, 12) for left sleeve, pm, k34 (34, 34, 36, 36, 36) for back, pm, k10 (10, 10, 12, 12, 12) for right sleeve, pm, k1 for right front.

INC ROW 1: (RS) K1f&b (see Glossary), slip marker (sl m), k1f&b, *knit to 1 st before m, k1f&b, sl m, k1f&b; rep from * 2 more times, knit to end—64 (64, 64, 70, 70, 70) sts.

NEXT ROW: (WS) Knit.

INC ROW 2: (RS) *Knit to 1 st before m, M1 (see Glossary), k1, sl m, k1, M1; rep from * 3 more times, knit to end—8 sts inc'd.

NEXT ROW: Knit to m, sl m, purl to last m, sl m, knit to end.

Rep last 2 rows 1 (1, 1, 3, 3, 3) more time(s)—80 (80, 80, 102, 102, 102) sts.

Cont working neck and raglan increases as foll:

ROW 1: (RS) K1f&b, *knit to 1 st before m, M1, k1, sl m, k1, M1; rep from * 3 times, knit to last st, k1f&b—10 sts inc'd.

ROWS 2 AND 4: Knit to m, sl m, purl to last m, sl m, knit to end.

ROW 3: *Knit to 1 st before m, M1, k1, sl m, k1, M1; rep from * 3 times, knit to end—98 (98, 98, 120, 120, 120) sts.

ROW 5: Rep Row 1—108 (108, 108, 130, 130, 130) sts.

ROW 6: K8 (8, 8, 10, 10, 10), purl to last 8 (8, 8, 10, 10, 10) sts, knit to end.

ROWS 7 AND 9: Rep Row 1—10 sts inc'd each row; 128 (128, 128, 150, 150, 150) sts after Row 9.

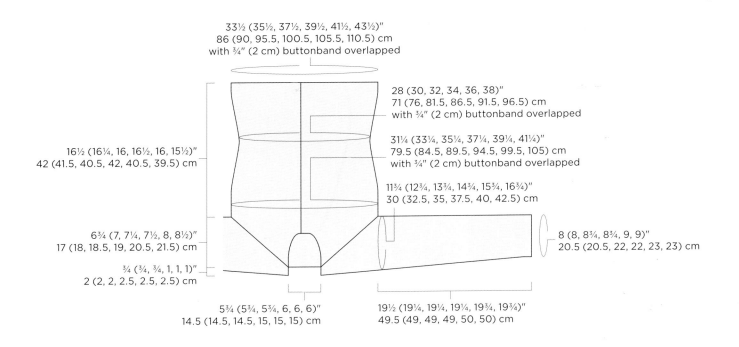

33½ (35½, 37½, 39½, 41½, 43½)"
86 (90, 95.5, 100.5, 105.5, 110.5) cm
with ¾" (2 cm) buttonband overlapped

28 (30, 32, 34, 36, 38)"
71 (76, 81.5, 86.5, 91.5, 96.5) cm
with ¾" (2 cm) buttonband overlapped

31¼ (33¼, 35¼, 37¼, 39¼, 41¼)"
79.5 (84.5, 89.5, 94.5, 99.5, 105) cm
with ¾" (2 cm) buttonband overlapped

16½ (16¼, 16, 16½, 16, 15½)"
42 (41.5, 40.5, 42, 40.5, 39.5) cm

11¾ (12¾, 13¾, 14¾, 15¾, 16¾)"
30 (32.5, 35, 37.5, 40, 42.5) cm

8 (8, 8¾, 8¾, 9, 9)"
20.5 (20.5, 22, 22, 23, 23) cm

6¾ (7, 7¼, 7½, 8, 8½)"
17 (18, 18.5, 19, 20.5, 21.5) cm

¾ (¾, ¾, 1, 1, 1)"
2 (2, 2, 2.5, 2.5, 2.5) cm

5¾ (5¾, 5¾, 6, 6, 6)"
14.5 (14.5, 14.5, 15, 15, 15) cm

19½ (19¼, 19¼, 19¼, 19¾, 19¾)"
49.5 (49, 49, 49, 50, 50) cm

ROW 8: K9 (9, 9, 11, 11, 11), purl to last 9 (9, 9, 11, 11, 11) sts, knit to end.

ROW 10: K10 (10, 10, 12, 12, 12), purl to last 10 (10, 10, 12, 12, 12) sts, knit to end.

Cont for your size as foll:

SIZES 37¼, 39¼, 41¼" ONLY
ROW 11: Rep Row 1—160 sts.

ROW 12: K13, purl to last 13 sts, knit to end.

ALL SIZES
ROWS 11 (11, 11, 13, 13, 13), 13 (13, 13, 15, 15, 15), AND 15 (15, 15, 17, 17, 17): Rep Row 1—10 sts inc'd each row.

ROW 12 (12, 12, 14, 14, 14): K1f&b, k10 (10, 10, 13, 13, 13), purl to last 11 (11, 11, 14, 14, 14) sts, knit to last st, k1f&b—140 (140, 140, 172, 172, 172) sts.

ROW 14 (14, 14, 16, 16, 16): K1f&b, k12 (12, 12, 15, 15, 15), purl to last 13 (13, 13, 16, 16, 16) sts, knit to last st, k1f&b—152 (152, 152, 184, 184, 184) sts.

ROW 16 (16, 16, 18, 18, 18): K1f&b, k14 (14, 14, 17, 17, 17), purl to last 15 (15, 15, 18, 18, 18) sts, knit to last st, k1f&b, use the knitted method (see Glossary) to CO 8 sts for center front neck—172 (172, 172, 204, 204, 204) sts.

ROW 17 (17, 17, 19, 19, 19): Knit the 8 newly CO sts through their back loops (tbl), *knit to 1 st before m, M1, k1, sl m, k1, M1; rep from * 3 times, knit to end, then use the knitted method to CO 8 sts as before—188 (188, 188, 220, 220, 220) sts.

NOTE: Buttonholes are introduced while raglan shaping is in progress; read all the way through the foll section before proceeding.

Rep the last 2 rows 10 (12, 15, 13, 16, 18) more times and *at the same time* on the first RS row, make the first buttonhole as described in the Note on page 108—276 (292, 316, 332, 356, 372) sts total: 42 (44, 47, 49, 52, 54) sts for each front, 80 (84, 90, 94, 100, 104) sts for back, 56 (60, 66, 70, 76, 80) sts for each sleeve.

Work even until piece measures 6¾ (7, 7¼, 7½, 8, 8½)" (17 [18, 18.5, 19, 20.5, 21.5] cm) from CO at back neck edge, ending with a WS row.

Divide for Armholes

With RS facing, *knit to first m, remove m, place 56 (60, 66, 70, 76, 80) sleeve sts onto waste yarn holder, remove second m, use the knitted method to CO 14 (16, 16, 18, 18, 20) sts and place marker (pm) in the center of these CO sts; rep from * once, knit to end—192 (204, 216, 228, 240, 252) sts rem for body.

Body

Working buttonholes as established, cont as foll:

ROW 1: (WS) K23 (23, 23, 26, 26, 26), purl to last 23 (23, 23, 26, 26, 26) sts, knit to end.

ROW 2 AND ALL RS ROWS: Knit.

ROW 3: K22 (22, 22, 25, 25, 25), purl to last 22 (22, 22, 25, 25, 25) sts, knit to end.

ROW 5: K21 (21, 21, 24, 24, 24), purl to last 21 (21, 21, 24, 24, 24) sts, knit to end.

ROW 18 (18, 18, 20, 20, 20): K24 (24, 24, 27, 27, 27), purl to last 24 (24, 24, 27, 27, 27) sts, knit to end.

ROW 19 (19, 19, 21, 21, 21): *Knit to 1 st before m, M1, k1, sl m, k1, M1; rep from * 3 times, knit to end—8 sts inc'd.

Rep Rows 14 and 15 until piece measures 3 (3, 3, 3, 2¾, 2½)" (7.5 [7.5, 7.5, 7.5, 7, 6.5] cm) from dividing row, ending with a WS row.

Shape Waist

DEC ROW: (RS) *Knit to 3 sts before marker, ssk, k1, sl m, k1, k2tog; rep from * once, knit to end of row—4 sts dec'd.

Work 9 (9, 9, 7, 7, 7) rows even. Rep the last 10 (10, 10, 8, 8, 8) rows 4 more times—172 (184, 196, 208, 220, 232) sts rem.

Work even until piece measures 10 (10, 9¾, 9¾, 9½, 9)" (25.5 [25.5, 25, 25, 24, 23] cm) from dividing row, ending with a WS row.

INC ROW: (RS) *Knit to 2 sts before m, M1, k2, sl m, k2, M1; rep from * once, knit to end of row—4 sts inc'd.

Work 3 rows even. Rep the last 4 rows 5 more times—196 (208, 220, 232, 244, 256) sts.

Work even as established until a total of 7 buttonholes have been made, followed by 3 garter ridges on the RS (6 rows), ending with a WS row.

Ribbing

SET-UP ROW: (RS) K4, *k1, p1; rep from * to last 4 sts, k4.

Cont in rib as established until a total of 8 buttonholes have been made, followed by 4 more rows of rib.

Use the sewn method (see Glossary) to BO all sts.

ROW 7: K20 (20, 20, 23, 23, 23), purl to last 20 (20, 20, 23, 23, 23) sts, knit to end.

ROW 9: K18 (18, 18, 21, 21, 21), purl to last 18 (18, 18, 21, 21, 21) sts, knit to end.

ROW 11: K16 (16, 16, 19, 19, 19), purl to last 16 (16, 16, 19, 19, 19) sts, knit to end.

ROW 13: K14 (14, 14, 17, 17, 17), purl to last 14 (14, 14, 17, 17, 17) sts, knit to end.

ROW 14: Knit.

ROW 15: K4, purl to last 4 sts, knit to end.

Sleeves

Place 56 (60, 66, 70, 76, 80) held sleeve sts onto 3 or 4 dpn. With RS facing, rejoin yarn and pick up and knit 16 (18, 18, 20, 20, 22) sts along CO edge at underarm (picking up 1 additional st on each side of CO sts to prevent gaps), placing a removable m at the center of picked-up sts to denote beg of rnd—72 (78, 84, 90, 96, 102) sts total.

DEC RND 1: K2tog, knit to last 2 sts, ssk—70 (76, 82, 88, 94, 100) sts rem.

Knit 7 (10, 16, 10, 20, 25) rnds even.

DEC RND 2: K1, k2tog, knit to 3 sts before m, ssk, k1—2 sts dec'd.

Knit 11 (8, 7, 6, 5, 4) rnds even.

Rep the last 12 (9, 8, 7, 6, 5) rnds 10 (13, 14, 17, 19, 22) more times—48 (48, 52, 52, 54, 54) sts rem; piece measures about 17½ (17¼, 17¼, 17¼, 17¾, 17¾)" (44.5 [44, 44, 44, 45, 45] cm) from pick-up rnd.

NEXT RND: *K1, p1; rep from *.

Work rib as established for 2" (5 cm).

Use the sewn method to BO all sts.

Finishing

Crochet Scallop

With crochet hook, work 1 row of crochet chain st (see Glossary for crochet instructions) along the outer edge of the garter st bib of yoke and along the garter st trim of neck edge.

Beg at right buttonband, work 1 sc in first st, *ch 5, skip 2 sts if working horizontally (skip 3 rows if working vertically), 1 sc in the next st; rep from * to end.

Fasten off.

Sew buttons to buttonband, opposite buttonholes. Weave in loose ends. Steam-block lightly.

FINISHED SIZE

About 26¾ (29, 31½, 33¾, 36¼, 38¾, 41, 43½, 45¾)" (68 [73.5, 80, 85.5, 92, 98.5, 104, 110.5, 116] cm) waistband circumference, 32¼ (35, 38, 41, 43¾, 46¾, 49¾, 52½, 55½)" (82 [89, 96.5, 104, 111, 118.5, 126.5, 133.5, 141] cm) hip circumference measured about 5" (20.5 cm) below top of waistband, and 20½" (52 cm) long from lower edge of waistband (for all sizes).

Skirt shown measures 31½" (80 cm) at waist.

YARN

Sportweight (#2 Fine).

Shown here: The Fibre Company Savannah (50% wool, 20% cotton, 15% linen, 15% soya; 160 yd [146 m]/50 g): bluegrass, 6 (7, 7, 8, 8, 9, 9, 10, 10) skeins.

NEEDLES

Sizes U.S. 4, 5, 6, and 7 (3.5, 3.75, 4, and 4.5 mm): 24" (60 cm) circular (cir) for each size.

Adjust needle size if necessary to obtain the correct gauge.

NOTIONS

Marker (m); 1" (2.5 cm) wide elastic to fit around waist plus 1" (2.5 cm) overlap; tapestry needle; sharp-point sewing needle and thread to sew elastic.

GAUGE

22 sts and 30 rnds = 4" (10 cm) in St st on size 5 (second from smallest size) needle, worked in rnds.

24 sts and 31 rnds = 4" (10 cm) in St st on size 4 (smallest size) needle, worked in rnds.

BARTON SPRINGS SKIRT

DESIGNED BY *Cecily Glowik MacDonald*

November in Austin always makes me think of heading down to Zilker Park and enjoying the autumn sunshine at Barton Springs. This season-spanning skirt is a great way to show off handknits in a warmer climate, where just a bit of wool is needed to take off the chill. Knitted from the bottom up, progressively smaller needles are used to create a fitted silhouette. The ruffles are knitted separately, then joined to the body of the skirt without seaming for minimal finishing. Pair this skirt with leather boots and your favorite jean jacket, and you'll be ready for anything!

NOTE

❖ The skirt begins at the lower edge with the ruffle and lace patterns worked on the largest needle. It is shaped by changing to progressively smaller needles to the ribbed waist, which is worked on the smallest size.

Skirt

With largest (size U.S. 7) needle, CO 354 (386, 418, 450, 482, 514, 546, 578, 610) sts. Do not join.

Knit 1 WS row. Change to St st (knit RS rows; purl WS rows) and work even until piece measures 2″ (5 cm) from CO, ending with a WS row.

DEC ROW: (RS) Change to next smaller (size U.S. 6) needle and work *k2tog; rep from *—177 (193, 209, 225, 241, 257, 273, 289, 305) sts rem.

SET UP FOR RIB TRIM FOR BACK SLIT: (WS) [P1, k1] 2 times, work in St st to last 4 sts, [k1, p1] 2 times.

Work even in patt as established until piece measures 1½″ (3.8 cm) from dec row, ending with a WS row.

PURL RIDGE: (RS) Work 4 sts in rib as established, purl to last 4 sts, work in rib to end.

Working the first 4 and last 4 sts in rib as established, cont in St st until piece measures 1½″ (3.8 cm) from purl ridge, ending with a WS row.

Rep purl ridge.

Working the first 4 and last 4 sts in rib as established, cont in St st until piece measures 6″ (15 cm) from CO, ending with a RS row.

JOINING RND: Place marker (pm) to denote beg of rnd and join for working in rnds.

Working rib as established, cont in rnds until piece measures 1″ (2.5 cm) from joining rnd.

Work all sts in St st until piece measures 11″ (28 cm) from CO.

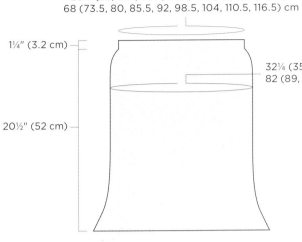

26¾ (29, 31½, 33¾, 36¼, 38¾, 41, 43½, 45¾)"
68 (73.5, 80, 85.5, 92, 98.5, 104, 110.5, 116.5) cm

1¼" (3.2 cm)

32¼ (35, 38, 41, 43¾, 46¾, 49¾, 52½, 55½)"
82 (89, 96.5, 104, 111, 118.5, 126.5, 133.5, 141) cm

20½" (52 cm)

Change to next smaller (size U.S. 5) needle and work even in St st until piece measures 17½" (44.5 cm) from CO.

Change to smallest (size U.S. 4) needle and work even in St st until piece measures 20½" (52 cm) from CO.

Waistband and Facing

DEC RND: P3 (1, 4, 2, 0, 3, 1, 4, 2), [p2tog, p8] 17 (19, 20, 22, 24, 25, 27, 28, 30) times, p4 (2, 5, 3, 1, 4, 2, 5, 3)—160 (174, 189, 203, 217, 232, 246, 261, 275) sts rem.

Work even in St st until piece measures 1¼" (3.2 cm) from dec rnd.

NEXT RND: (turning ridge) P0 (2, 4, 1, 3, 1, 3, 0, 2), [p2tog, p8] 16 (17, 18, 20, 21, 23, 24, 26, 27) times, p0 (2, 5, 2, 4, 1, 3, 1, 3)—144 (157, 171, 183, 196, 209, 222, 235, 248) sts rem.

Knit 1 rnd.

☐	knit on RS, purl on WS
⊡	purl on RS, knit on WS
⊙	yo
⧅	ssk
⧄	k2tog
▣	pattern repeat

LACE RUFFLE

MESH RUFFLE

Remove m, turn work so WS is facing, and work St st in rows until facing measures 1¼" (3.2 cm) from turning ridge.

Loosely BO all sts.

Finishing

Mesh Ruffle

With largest (size U.S. 7) needle, CO 168 (184, 200, 216, 232, 248, 264, 280, 296) sts. Do not join.

Beg with a WS row, work Mesh Ruffle chart until piece measures 1¾" (4.5 cm) from CO, ending with a WS row. Work 2 rows even in St st.

JOIN RUFFLE TO BODY

BO all sts while working as foll: With sts still on needle and RS facing, use left-hand needle to pick up top bump of the first purl st of the first purl ridge on the body of skirt and knit this st together with the first st on the needle as k2tog. Rep with the top of each purl bump and the next st on the needle to end of sts.

Lace Ruffle

With largest (size U.S. 7) needle, CO 173 (191, 200, 218, 236, 254, 272, 281, 299) sts. Do not join.

Work in Lace Ruffle chart until piece measures 1¾" 4.5 cm) from CO, ending with a RS row.

SIZES 26¾ (29, 33¾, 36¼, 38¾, 41, 43½, 45¾)" ONLY

DEC ROW: (WS) P11 (11, 60, 30, 21, 16, 140, 46) sts, [p2tog, p35 (26, 94, 56, 40, 32, 0, 101] 4 (6, 1, 3, 5, 7, 0, 2) times, p2tog, p12 (10, 60, 30, 21, 16, 140, 46)—168 (184, 216, 232, 248, 264, 280, 296) sts rem.

SIZE 31½" ONLY

NEXT ROW: (WS) Purl.

ALL SIZES

Join to second purl ridge as described for mesh ruffle.

Block to measurements. Fold facing to WS along turning ridge and, with yarn threaded on a tapestry needle, sew BO edge of facing to inside of skirt to form casing for elastic. Thread elastic through casing, overlap ends as necessary to achieve the correct fit, then use sharp-point sewing needle and thread to sew the overlapped ends of the elastic together. With yarn threaded on a tapestry needle, sew selvedges of facing tog to close opening in casing.

Weave in loose ends. Block again, if desired.

FINISHED SIZE
About 43" (109 cm) around opening.

YARN
Worsted weight (#4 Medium).

Shown here: The Fibre Company Road to China Worsted (65% alpaca, 10% cashmere, 10% camel, 15% silk; 69 yd [63 m]/50 g): carnelian, 7 skeins.

NEEDLES
Ribbing: size U.S. 9 (5.5 mm): 24" and 16" (60 and 40 cm) circular (cir).

Body: size U.S. 10 (6 mm): straight or 24" (60 cm) cir and 2 double-pointed (dpn).

Adjust needle size if necessary to obtain the correct gauge.

NOTIONS
Smooth waste yarn of comparable gauge for provisional cast-on; tapestry needle.

GAUGE
12 sts and 20 rows = 4" (10 cm) in lace patt on larger needles.

12 sts and 28 rows = 4" (10 cm) in k2, p2 rib on smaller needles.

TALLULAH SHRUG

DESIGNED BY *Courtney Kelley*

Having grown up in a southern climate, I often find myself as underdressed for fall as the trees are. For the first few years that I lived in the northeast, I resented the way I had to give up comfortable layers in favor of a frumpy and uninspiring winter coat. Designed to be warm enough on days when a cardigan and jean jacket just won't cut it, this shrug is elegant enough to give my wardrobe a bit of flattering fashion. The Road to China yarn is a luxurious worsted-weight blend of alpaca, cashmere, camel, and silk that creates beautiful drape, softness, and warmth.

Body

With larger needles use a provisional method (see Glossary) to CO 84 sts. Do not join. Work Rows 1–6 of Lace chart 15 times.

Sleeves

Carefully remove waste yarn from provisional CO row and place 84 exposed sts onto smaller cir needle. Fold body in half with WS facing each other and so that the needles are parallel. Place the first 7 sts of each needle onto a larger dpn and, with yarn threaded on a tapestry needle, use the Kitchener st (see Glossary) to graft these sts tog. Rep on other side for other sleeve.

Finishing

Body Edging

With smaller cir needle and RS facing, work 70 sts from larger needle in k2, p2 rib, then work rem 70 sts in rib as established—140 sts total. Work in rib as established until edging measures 5" (12.5 cm).

With larger needles, loosely BO all sts.

Sleeve Edging

With smaller cir needle and RS facing, pick up and knit 52 sts evenly spaced around sleeve opening. Pm and join for working in rnds. Work in k2, p2 rib for 2" (5 cm).

Loosely BO all sts. Rep for other sleeve.

Weave in loose ends. Block to measurements.

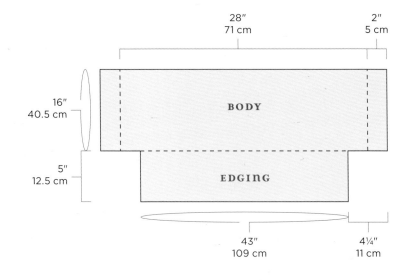

28"
71 cm

2"
5 cm

16"
40.5 cm

BODY

5"
12.5 cm

EDGING

43"
109 cm

4¼"
11 cm

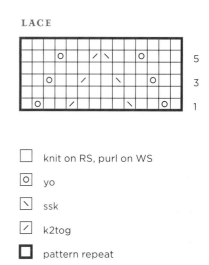

LACE

		O			╱	╲			O			5
	O			╱			╲			O		3
O			╱					╲			O	1

☐ knit on RS, purl on WS

⊡ yo

╲ ssk

╱ k2tog

◻ pattern repeat

Tallulah Shrug

FINISHED SIZE

About 30 (34½, 38¼, 41¾, 45¼, 48¾, 52¼)" (76 [87.5, 97, 106, 115, 124, 132.5] cm) bust circumference, buttoned.

Cardigan shown measures 34½" (87.5 cm).

YARN

Worsted weight (#4 Medium).

Shown here: Quince and Company Lark (100% American wool; 134 yd [123 m]/50 g): 104 storm, 8 (8, 9, 10, 11, 12, 13) skeins.

NEEDLES

Body and sleeves: size U.S. 8 (5 mm): straight and 32" (80 cm) circular (cir).

Edging: size U.S. 7 (4.5 mm): straight and 32" (80 cm) cir.

Adjust needle size if necessary to obtain the correct gauge.

NOTIONS

Markers (m); stitch holders or waste yarn; tapestry needle; six ½" (1.3 cm) buttons.

GAUGE

18 sts and 27 rows= 4" (10 cm) in St st on larger needles.

18 sts and 32 rows = 4" (10 cm) in garter ladder st (stretched) on smaller needles.

ABILENE CARDIGAN

DESIGNED BY *Carrie Bostick Hoge*

November is a beautiful month with a crispness in the air that calls for wearing something warm and pretty. I imagine the perfect sweater to be a cardigan made from soft local wool with simple construction and a few lacey details—something just like this cardigan. Knitted from the bottom up in one piece, the body has side shaping for an attractive fit and a bit of lace for interest at the cuffs and yoke. Inspired by a vintage cardigan that has been a well-loved staple in my own wardrobe, this version is versatility at it's best—it can be dressed up or down.

Stitch Guide

**Garter Ladder Stitch:
(multiple of 4 sts)**

ROW 1: (RS) *K2tog, [yo] 2 times, ssk; rep from *.

ROW 2: *K1, (k1, p1) into double yo, k1; rep from *.

Rep Rows 1 and 2 for patt.

Body

With smaller cir needle, CO 134 (150, 166, 182, 198, 214, 230) sts. Do not join.

ROW 1: (RS) Knit.

ROW 2: P1, knit to last st, p1.

Rep Rows 1 and 2 until piece measures about 2" (5 cm) from CO, ending with a WS row.

Change to larger cir needle and work even in St st (knit RS rows; purl WS rows) until piece measures about 4" (10 cm) from CO, ending with a RS row.

NEXT ROW: (WS) P32 (36, 40, 44, 48, 52, 56) for left front, place marker (pm), p70 (78, 86, 94, 102, 110, 118) for back, pm, p32 (36, 40, 44, 48, 52, 56) for right front.

Shape Waist

DEC ROW: (RS) *Knit to 4 sts before m, ssk, k2, sl m, k2, k2tog; rep from * once, knit to end—4 sts dec'd.

Work 11 rows even, then rep dec row, then work 9 rows even, then rep dec row again—122 (138, 154, 170, 186, 202, 218) sts rem.

Cont even in St st until piece measures 9¼" (23.5 cm) from CO, ending with a WS row.

INC ROW: (RS) *Knit to 2 sts before m, M1 (see Glossary), k2, sl m, k2, M1; rep from * once, knit to end—4 sts inc'd.

Work 9 rows even, then rep inc row, then work 11 rows even, then rep inc row again—134 (150, 166, 182, 198, 214, 230) sts. Cont even in St st until piece measures 13 (13¼, 14, 14, 14, 15, 15)" (33 [33.5, 35.5, 35.5,

knit on RS, purl on WS

• purl on RS, knit on WS

／ k2tog

＼ ssk

○ yo

▢ pattern repeat

GARTER LADDER

	•	•	
＼	○	○	／

1

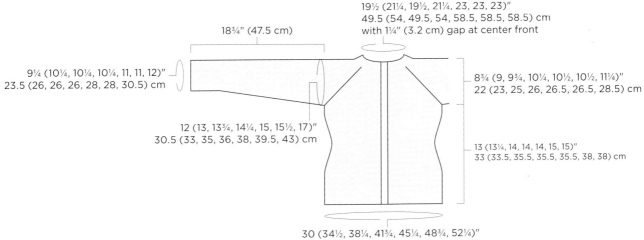

19½ (21¼, 19½, 21¼, 23, 23, 23)"
49.5 (54, 49.5, 54, 58.5, 58.5, 58.5) cm
with 1¼" (3.2 cm) gap at center front

18¾" (47.5 cm)

9¼ (10¼, 10¼, 10¼, 11, 11, 12)"
23.5 (26, 26, 26, 28, 28, 30.5) cm

8¾ (9, 9¾, 10¼, 10½, 10½, 11¼)"
22 (23, 25, 26, 26.5, 26.5, 28.5) cm

12 (13, 13¾, 14¼, 15, 15½, 17)"
30.5 (33, 35, 36, 38, 39.5, 43) cm

13 (13¼, 14, 14, 14, 15, 15)"
33 (33.5, 35.5, 35.5, 35.5, 38, 38) cm

30 (34½, 38¼, 41¾, 45¼, 48¾, 52¼)"
76 (87.5, 97, 106, 115, 124, 132.5) cm
with 1¼" (3.2 cm) gap at center front

35.5, 38, 38] cm) from CO, ending with a RS row.

Divide for Fronts and Back

With WS facing, *purl to 4 sts before m, BO 8 sts, removing m when you come to it; rep from * once, purl to end—28 (32, 36, 40, 44, 48, 52) sts rem for each front, 62 (70, 78, 86, 94, 102, 110) sts rem for back. Do not cut yarn. Set aside.

Sleeves

With smaller straight needles, CO 42 (46, 46, 46, 50, 50, 54) sts.

ROW 1: (RS) Knit.

ROW 2: (WS) P1, knit to last st, p1.

Rep these 2 rows 2 more times.

Work garter ladder st as foll:

ROW 1: (RS) K1, work in garter ladder st (see Stitch Guide or chart on page 126) to last st, k1.

Cont in patt as established until piece measures 3" (7.5 cm) from CO, ending with a WS row.

NEXT ROW: (RS) Knit.

NEXT ROW: (WS) P1, knit to last st, p1.

Cont as established for 2 more rows.

Change to larger needles and work in St st until piece measures 4" (10 cm) from CO, ending with a WS row.

Shape Sleeve

INC ROW: (RS) K2, M1, knit to last 2 sts, M1, k2—2 sts inc'd.

Work 17 (17, 11, 11, 11, 9, 7) rows even.

Rep the last 18 (18, 12, 12, 12, 10, 8) rows 4 (4, 6, 7, 7, 8, 9) times, then rep inc row once more—54 (58, 62, 64, 68, 70, 76) sts.

Work even until piece measures 18¾" (47.5 cm) from CO, ending with a WS row.

BO 4 sts at beg of next 2 rows—46 (50, 54, 56, 60, 62, 68) sts rem.

Place sts on st holder or waste yarn, cut yarn, and set aside.

Yoke

JOINING ROW: (RS) With larger cir needle and yarn attached to body, k28 (32, 36, 40, 44, 48, 52) right front sts, pm, k46 (50, 54, 56, 60, 62, 68) sleeve sts, pm, k62 (70, 78, 86, 94, 102, 110) back sts, pm, k46 (50, 54, 56, 60, 62, 68) sleeve sts, pm, k28 (32, 36, 40, 44, 48, 52) left front sts—210 (234, 258, 278, 302, 322, 350) sts total.

Work 3 rows even in St st.

DEC ROW: (RS) *Knit to 3 sts before m, ssk, k1, sl m, k1, k2tog; rep from * 3 more times, knit to end—8 sts dec'd.

Work 3 rows even. Rep the last 4 rows 4 (3, 3, 3, 2, 1, 0) time(s), then rep dec row every RS row 2 (5, 9, 10, 13, 17, 21) times—154 (162, 154, 166, 174, 170, 174) sts rem.

Cont for your size as foll:

SIZES (41¾, 45¼, 52¼)" ONLY
Purl 1 WS row.

*Knit to 3 sts before m, ssk, k1, sl m, work to m, sl m, k1, k2tog; rep from * once, knit to end—(162, 170, 170) sts rem.

ALL SIZES
NEXT ROW: (WS) P1, knit to last st, p1.

NEXT ROW: (RS) *Knit to 3 sts before m, ssk, k1, sl m, k1, k2tog; rep from * 3 more times, knit to end—146 (154, 146, 154, 162, 162, 162) sts rem; 20 (22, 22, 24, 26, 28, 28) sts for each front; 30 (30, 26, 26, 26, 22, 22) sts for each sleeve; 46 (50, 50, 54, 58, 62, 62) sts for back.

NEXT ROW: (WS) P1, knit to last st, p1.

Change to smaller needle and work garter ladder st while shaping yoke as foll:

ROW 1: (RS) K3 (1, 1, 3, 1, 3, 3), *work Row 1 of garter ladder st to 5 sts before m, k2tog, yo, ssk, k1, sl m, k1, k2tog, yo, ssk; rep from 3 more times, work Row 1 of garter ladder st to last 3 (1, 1, 3, 1, 3, 3) st(s), k3 (1, 1, 3, 1, 3, 3)—138 (146, 138, 146, 154, 154, 154) sts rem.

ROW 2: (WS) P1, k2 (0, 0, 2, 0, 2, 2), *work Row 2 of garter ladder st to 4 sts before m, k4, sl m, k4; rep from * 3 more times, work in garter ladder st to last 3 (1, 1, 3, 1, 3, 3) st(s), k2 (0, 0, 2, 0, 2, 2), p1.

Working in patt as established, cont as foll:

ROW 3: *Work to 4 sts before m, k2tog, k2, sl m, k2, ssk; rep from * 3 more times, work to end—130 (138, 130, 138, 146, 146, 146) sts rem.

ROW 4: *Work to 3 sts before m, k3, sl m, k3; rep from * 3 more times, work to end.

ROW 5: *Work to 3 sts before m, k2tog, k1, sl m, k1, ssk; rep from * 3 more times, work to end—122 (130, 122, 130, 138, 138, 138) sts rem.

ROW 6: *Work to 2 sts before m, k2, sl m, k2; rep from * 3 more times, work to end.

ROW 7: *Work to 2 sts before m, k2tog, sl m, ssk; rep from * 3 more times, work to end—114 (122, 114, 122, 130, 130, 130) sts rem.

ROW 8: *Work to 1 st before m, k1, sl m, k1; rep from * 3 more times, work to end.

Rep Rows 1–8 once more—82 (90, 82, 90, 98, 98, 98) sts rem.

Neckband

With smaller cir needle, work even in garter st (knit every row) for 1″ (2.5 cm), ending with a RS row.

With WS facing, BO all sts knitwise.

Finishing

Weave in loose ends. Block to measurements.

With yarn threaded on a tapestry needle, sew sleeve and underarm seams.

Buttonhole Band

With smaller cir needle, RS facing, and beg at lower edge of right front, pick up and knit 100 (110, 114, 116, 116, 120, 120) sts evenly spaced to neck edge. Work in garter st for 3 rows, ending with a WS row.

BUTTONHOLE ROW: (RS) K4 (4, 8, 10, 10, 9, 9), k2tog, yo, *k16 (18, 18, 18, 18, 19, 19), k2tog, yo; rep from * 4 more times, end k4.

Work in garter st for 6 more rows, ending with a RS row. With WS facing, BO all sts knitwise.

Buttonband

With smaller cir needle, RS facing, and beg at neck edge of left front, pick up and knit 100 (110, 114, 116, 116, 120, 120) sts evenly spaced to lower edge. Work in garter st for 10 rows, ending with a RS row. With WS facing, BO all sts knitwise.

Sew buttons to left front, opposite buttonholes.

FINISHED SIZE

About 10" (25.5 cm) wide and
64" (162.5 cm) long.

YARN

Sportweight (#2 Fine).

Shown here: Schaefer Yarn Audrey (50% wool, 50% silk; 700 yd
[640 m]/112 g): thistle, 1 skein.

NEEDLES

Size U.S. 6 (4 mm).

*Adjust needle size if necessary
to obtain the correct gauge.*

NOTIONS

Waste yarn or stitch holder; 2,012
size 8° glass seed beads (about
60 grams); dental floss threader
for threading beads; tapestry
needle.

GAUGE

31 sts and 24 rows = 4" (10 cm)
in charted pattern.

BLUEBONNET SCARF

DESIGNED BY *Laura Nelkin*

This fanciful scarf is designed for beauty as well as warmth.
It is wide enough to function as either a scarf or a shawl. Wrap
it around your neck as you head out on a blustery day and then
rearrange it over your shoulders to arrive at your destination
in style. Purl stitches delineate separate panels of lace motifs, adding dimensionality to the fabric and acting as built-in
stitch markers to help keep the separate lace sections on track.
Worked in two halves that are grafted together, the bottom
edges match perfectly!

NOTES

✦ Thread yarn through large loop at bottom of dental floss threader leaving about 6" (15 m) tail, then pick up beads with the threader and slide them down onto the yarn.

✦ A yo with beads is correctly mounted if the right leg (the leading leg) of the yo is to the front of the needle and the left leg is to the back. When the beaded yo from the previous row comes *after* a yo on the current row, the beads should be to the *front* of the left-hand needle as the new yo is worked; when the beaded yo from the previous row comes *before* a yo on the current row, the beads should be to the *back* of the left-hand needle as the new yo is worked.

Stitch Guide

MAKE A YO WITH BEADS: Slide beads up yarn so that they sit directly next to the right needle tip. Bring yarn from front to back over needle to form a yo while sliding the specified number of beads into place, then work the next st as directed. The beads will be held in place on the yo.

Scarf

First Half

Thread 504 beads onto yarn (see Notes).

Using the knitted method (see Glossary), CO 77 sts.

Work Rows 1–24 of Bead and Lace chart 4 times, moving beads into place as specified on chart.

Cut yarn, thread on 504 more beads, then work Rows 1–24 of chart 4 more times— 8 patt reps total; piece measures about 32" (81.5 cm) from CO.

Place sts on waste yarn, cut yarn, and set aside.

Second Half

Work as for first half, ending after Row 23 of the 8th patt rep.

Leave sts on needle.

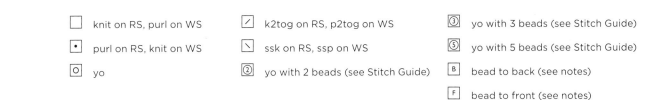

- knit on RS, purl on WS
- • purl on RS, knit on WS
- O yo
- / k2tog on RS, p2tog on WS
- \ ssk on RS, ssp on WS
- ② yo with 2 beads (see Stitch Guide)
- ③ yo with 3 beads (see Stitch Guide)
- ⑤ yo with 5 beads (see Stitch Guide)
- B bead to back (see notes)
- F bead to front (see notes)

BEADED LACE

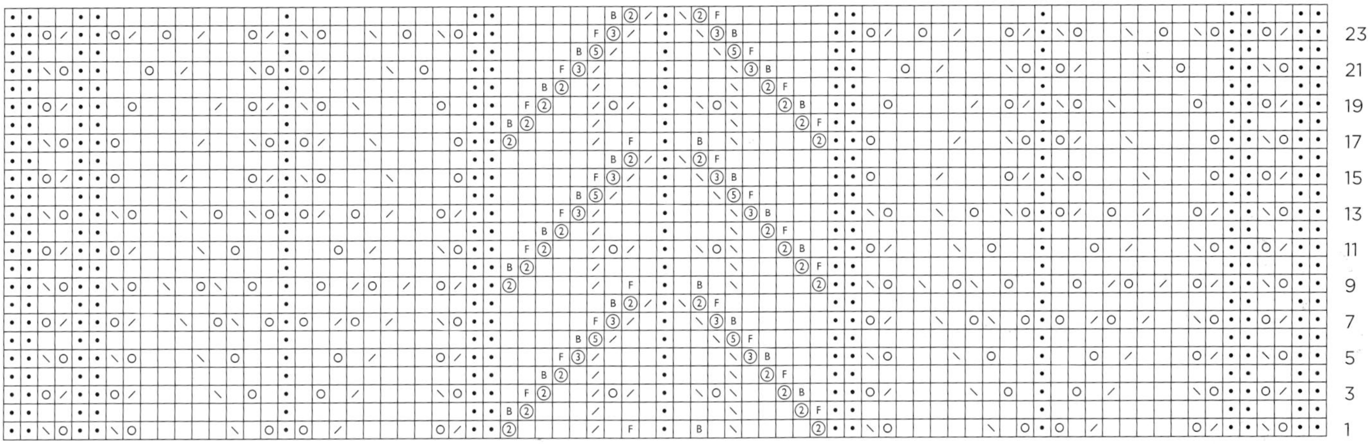

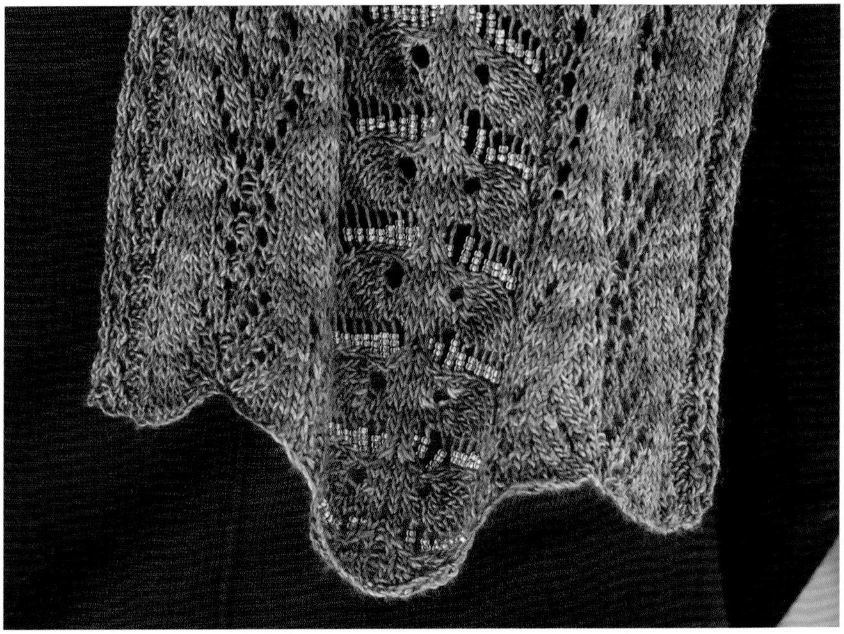

Finishing

Cut yarn, leaving a 40" (100 cm) tail. Return 77 held sts to one needle tip. Hold the pieces with WS facing tog and RS facing out. With tail threaded on tapestry needle use the Kitchener st (see Glossary) to graft the live sts tog.

Weave in loose ends. Block to measurements.

FINISHED SIZE

Tam: about 16" (40.5 cm) circumference at brim; will stretch to 21" (53.5 cm).

Scarf: about 6" (15 cm) wide and 59" (150 cm) long.

YARN

Fingering weight (#1 Super Fine).

Shown here: Madeline Tosh Sock (100% superwash merino; 395 yd [361 m]/100 g): composition book grey, 2 skeins.

NEEDLES

Tam: size U.S. 2 (2.75 mm): 16" (40 cm) circular (cir) and set of 4 or 5 double-pointed (dpn).

Scarf: size U.S. 3 (3.5 mm).

Adjust needle size if necessary to obtain the correct gauge.

NOTIONS

Smooth, contrasting color waste yarn of comparable gauge for tubular cast-on; marker (m); stitch holder or waste yarn; tapestry needle.

GAUGE

Tam: 34 sts and 44 rnds = 4" (10 cm) in lace pattern with smaller needles, worked in rnds, after blocking.

Scarf: 30 sts and 44 rows = 4" (10 cm) with larger needles in lace pattern, after blocking.

25 sts = 4" (10 cm) in k1, p1 rib with smaller needles, worked in rnds.

MOCKINGBIRD TAM & SCARF

DESIGNED BY *Kristen TenDyke*

This lacey set is as fun to knit as it is to wear. The tam begins with a tubular cast-on to provide a stretchy brim and then stitches are increased to create the slightly slouchy shape. The scarf is worked in two halves, each from the end to the center, then grafted together. The subtle variegation in the yarn provides beautiful color depth and visual interest. Because the stitch pattern is easy to memorize, both projects make good companions during holiday travels.

Tam

With waste yarn and smaller needles, use the tubular method worked in rnds (see Glossary) to CO 100 sts.

Edging

*K1, p1; rep from *.

Cont in rib as established until piece measures 1¼" (3.2 cm) from CO.

Body

RND 1: (inc rnd) *Yo, k1, p1, k1, yo, k1; rep from *—150 sts.

RND 2: *K2, p1, k3; rep from *.

RND 3: (inc rnd) K1, yo, *k3, yo; rep from * to last 2 sts, k2—200 sts.

RNDS 4-6: Knit.

Work Rnds 1–12 of Tam Lace chart 3 times, then work Rnds 1–5 once more.

NEXT RND: *K40, place marker (pm); rep from *—5 markers placed; one rep of dec chart will be worked between each set of markers.

Shape Crown

Work Rnds 1–30 of Tam Decrease chart— 5 sts rem.

TAM LACE

TAM DECREASE

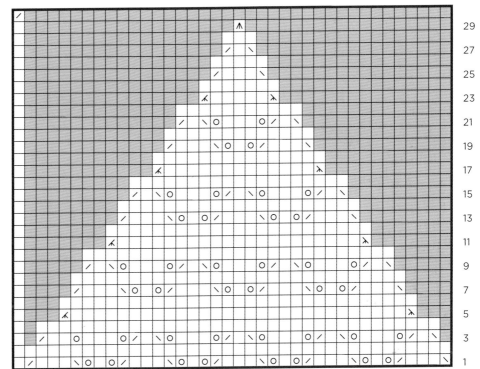

knit on RS, purl on WS

yo

k2tog

k3tog

ssk

sssk

slip 2 sts tog kwise, k1, p2sso

no stitch

pattern repeat

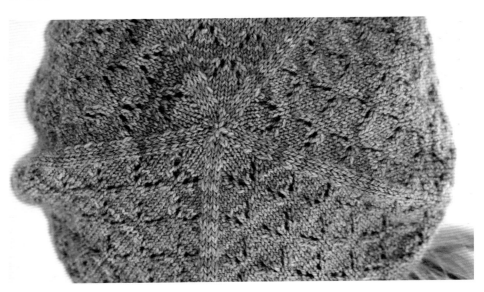

Mockingbird Tam & Scarf

Finishing

Cut yarn, leaving an 8″ (20.5 cm) tail. Thread tail onto a tapestry needle, draw through rem sts, pull tight to close hole, and fasten off on WS.

Soak in warm water and wool wash for 20 minutes, squeeze out water, lay flat and pin to 10″ (25.5 cm) circumference. Let air-dry thoroughly.

Scarf

First Half

With waste yarn and larger needles, use the tubular method worked in rows (see Glossary) to CO 69 sts.

NOTE: The RS of the tubular CO is the WS of the scarf.

EDGING

ROWS 1 AND 3: (WS) Sl 1 purlwise with yarn in front (pwise wyf), *p1, k1; rep from * to last 2 sts, p2.

ROW 2: (RS) Sl 1 pwise with yarn in back (wyb), *k1, p1; rep from * to last 2 sts, k2.

ROW 4: (dec row) Sl 1 pwise wyb, [k1, p1] 2 times, ssk, k1, [p1, k1] 3 times, k2tog, *k1, ssk, k1, [p1, k1] 3 times, k2tog; rep from * to last 5 sts, [p1, k1] 2 times, k1—59 sts rem.

ROW 5: Sl 1 pwise wyf, [p1, k1] 2 times, p2, [k1, p1] 3 times, *p4, [k1, p1] 3 times; rep from * to last 6 sts, [p1, k1] 2 times, p2.

ROW 6: (dec row) Sl 1 pwise wyb, k1, [p1, k1] 2 times, ssk, k3, k2tog, *k3, ssk, k3, k2tog; rep from * to last 6 sts, [k1, p1] 2 times, k2—49 sts rem.

SCARF LACE

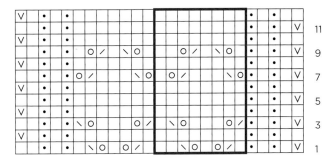

knit on RS, purl on WS

purl on RS, knit on WS

sl 1 pwise wyb on RS, wyf on WS

O yo

/ k2tog

\ ssk

pattern repeat

ROW 7: (WS) Sl 1 pwise wyf, [p1, k1] 2 times, purl to last 5 sts, [k1, p1] 2 times, p1.

BODY

Work Rows 1–12 of Scarf Lace chart 26 times, then work Rows 1–5 once more.

Place all sts onto a holder or waste yarn. Cut yarn.

Second Half

Work as for first half, but leave sts on needle. Cut yarn, leaving a 24" (61 cm) tail.

Finishing

Place held sts from first half onto an empty needle and hold the two pieces tog with the needles parallel and so that WS of fabric face tog and both needle tips face to the right. Thread tail on a tapestry needle and use the Kitchener st (see Glossary) to graft sts tog.

Weave in loose ends. Block to measurements.

FINISHED SIZE

About 10¾" (27.5 cm) circumference and 18" (45.5 cm) long.

YARN

Fingering weight (#1 Super Fine).

Shown here: The Fibre Company, Canopy Fingering (50% baby alpaca, 30% merino wool, 20% bamboo; 200 yd [183 m]/50 g): aloe, 2 skeins (with just a few yards left over).

NEEDLES

Ribbing: size U.S. 1 (2.25 mm): set of 5 double-pointed (dpn) or 9" (23 cm) circular (cir).

Leg: size U.S. 2 (2.75 mm): set of 5 dpn or 9" (23 cm) cir.

Adjust needle size if necessary to obtain the correct gauge.

NOTIONS

Markers (m), of which one is unique to denote end of rnd; tapestry needle.

GAUGE

28 sts and 36 rnds = 4" (10 cm) in Spanish Moss Lace chart on larger needles, worked in the rnd.

SPANISH MOSS LEG WARMERS

DESIGNED BY *Courtney Kelley*

Dresses and skirts are a staple of my wardrobe and leg warmers have always helped me with that awkward transition from summer dresses to winter skirts and sweaters. In areas with long and drawn-out fall seasons, it's great to have a lot of small accessories—like these leg warmers—to take the chill off a sunny day or to brighten a cool rainy one. The delicate lace pattern and open stitches allow the fabric to breathe, and the blend of wool, alpaca, and bamboo in the yarn provides welcome insulation. Fancy enough to wear to Sunday dinner, you'll want to keep these handy all year round.

NOTE

❖ The Spanish Moss Lace chart is worked 4 times on each round. If using double-pointed needles, place 19 stitches (1 pattern repeat) on each needle. If using a circular needle, place a marker after every 19 stitches to denote individual pattern repeats.

Leg Warmer (make 2)

With smaller needle(s), CO 76 sts. If using dpn, divide sts evenly on 4 dpn or, if using cir needle, place marker (pm) of unique color, then and join for working in rnds, being careful not to twist sts.

SET-UP RND: *K1, p1; rep from *.

Cont in k1, p1 rib as established until piece measures 3" (7.5 cm) from CO.

Change to larger needle(s).

Work Rnds 1–12 of Spanish Moss Lace chart 9 times—piece measures about 15" (38 cm) from CO.

Change to smaller needle(s).

Work in k1, p1 rib for 3" (7.5 cm).

Loosely BO all sts.

Finishing

Weave in loose ends. Block to measurements.

knit

○ yo

╱ k2tog

╲ ssk

⋀ slip 2 tog kwise, k1, p2sso

▮ pattern repeat

SPANISH MOSS LACE

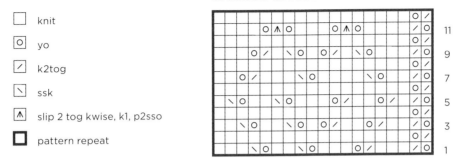

Spanish Moss Leg Warmers

143

GLOSSARY

Abbreviations

beg(s)	begin(s); beginning	p	purl	St st	stockinette stitch
BO	bind off	p1f&b	purl into front and back of same stitch	tbl	through back loop
cm	centimeter(s)	patt(s)	pattern(s)	tog	together
cn	cable needle	psso	pass slipped stitch over	WS	wrong side
CO	cast on	p2sso	pass 2 slipped stitches over	wyb	with yarn in back
cont	continue(s); continuing	pwise	purlwise, as if to purl	wyf	with yarn in front
dec(s)	decrease(s); decreasing	rem	remain(s); remaining	yd	yard(s)
dpn	double-pointed needles	rep	repeat(s); repeating	yo	yarnover
foll	follow(s); following	rev St st	reverse stockinette stitch	*	repeat starting point
g	gram(s)	rnd(s)	round(s)	**	repeat all instructions between asterisks
inc(s)	increase(s); increasing	RS	right side	( )	alternate measurements and/or instructions
k	knit	sl	slip	[ ]	work instructions as a group a specified number of times
k1f&b	knit into the front and back of same stitch	sl st	slip st (slip 1 stitch purlwise unless otherwise indicated)		
kwise	knitwise, as if to knit	ssk	slip, slip, knit (decrease)		
m	marker(s)	ssp	slip, slip, purl (decrease)		
mm	millimeter(s)	st(s)	stitch(es)		
M1	make one (increase)				

Bind-Offs

I-Cord Bind-Off

With right side facing and using the knitted method (see page 147), cast on 3 stitches (for cord) onto the end of the needle holding the stitches to be bound off (**FIGURE 1**), *k2, k2tog through back loops (the last cord stitch with the first stitch to be bound off; **FIGURE 2**), slip these 3 stitches back to the left needle (**FIGURE 3**), and pull the yarn firmly from the back. Repeat from * until 3 stitches remain on left needle and no stitches remain on right needle. Bind off remaining stitches using the standard method (shown at right).

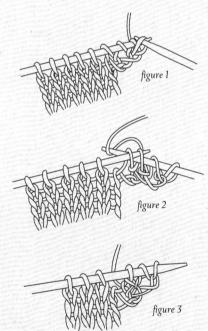

figure 1

figure 2

figure 3

Sewn Bind-Off

Cut the yarn, leaving a tail about four times the width or circumference of the knitting to be bound off, and thread the tail onto a tapestry needle.

Working from right to left, *insert the tapestry needle purlwise (from right to left) through the first 2 stitches on the left needle tip (**FIGURE 1**) and pull the yarn through. Bring tapestry needle through the first stitch again, but this time knitwise (from left to right; **FIGURE 2**), pull the yarn through, then slip this stitch off the knitting needle.

Repeat from * for the desired number of stitches.

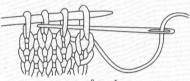

figure 1

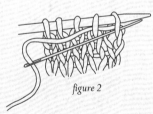

figure 2

Standard Bind-Off

Knit the first stitch, *knit the next stitch (2 stitches on right needle), insert left needle tip into first stitch on right needle (**FIGURE 1**) and lift this stitch up and over the second stitch (**FIGURE 2**) and off the needle (**FIGURE 3**). Repeat from * for the desired number of stitches.

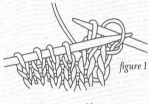

figure 1

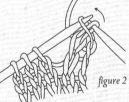

figure 2

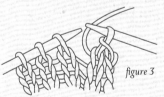

figure 3

Three-Needle Bind-Off

Place stitches to be joined onto two separate needles. Hold the needles parallel with right sides of knitting facing together, insert a third needle into the first stitch on each of the other two needles (FIGURE 1), and knit them together as 1 stitch (FIGURE 2). *Knit the next stitch on each needle together in the same way, then pass the first stitch over the second stitch and off the needle (FIGURE 3). Repeat from * until 1 stitch remains on third needle. Cut yarn and pull tail through last stitch to secure.

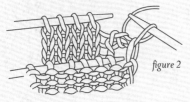

figure 1

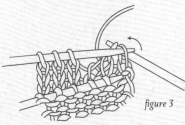

figure 2

figure 3

Buttonhole

NOTE: This one-row buttonhole is worked over 3 stitches.

Bring the yarn to the front of the work, slip the next stitch purlwise, then return the yarn to the back. *Slip the next stitch, pass the second stitch over the slipped stitch (FIGURE 1) and drop it off the needle. Repeat from * once more. Slip the last stitch on the right needle to the left needle, then turn the work

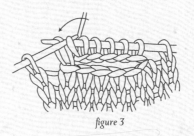

figure 1

figure 2

figure 3

around. Bring the working yarn to the back, [insert the right needle between the first and second stitches on the left needle (FIGURE 2), draw up a loop and place it on the left needle] three times. Turn the work around. With the yarn in back, slip the first stitch and pass the extra cast-on stitch over it (FIGURE 3) and off the needle to complete the buttonhole.

Cast-Ons

Backward-Loop Cast-On

*Loop working yarn and place it on needle backward so that it doesn't unwind. Repeat from *.

Cable Cast-On

If there are no stitches on the needles, make a slipknot of working yarn and place it on the needle, then use the knitted method (shown at right) to cast-on one more stitch—2 stitches on needle. Hold needle with working yarn in your left hand. *Insert right needle between the first 2 stitches on left needle (FIGURE 1), wrap yarn around needle as if to knit, draw yarn through (FIGURE 2), and place new loop on left needle (FIGURE 3) to form a new stitch. Repeat from * for the desired number of stitches, always working between the first 2 stitches on the left needle.

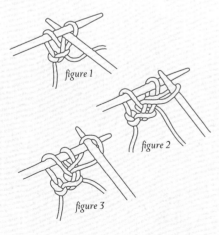

figure 1

figure 2

figure 3

Knitted Cast-On

Make a slipknot of working yarn and place it on the left needle if there are no stitches already there. *Use the right needle to knit the first stitch (or slipknot) on left needle (FIGURE 1) and place new loop onto left needle to form a new stitch (FIGURE 2). Repeat from * for the desired number of stitches, always working into the last stitch made.

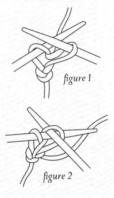

figure 1

figure 2

Long-Tail (Continental) Cast-On

Leaving a long tail (about ½" [1.3 cm] for each stitch to be cast on), make a slipknot and place on right needle. Place thumb and index finger of your left hand between the yarn ends so that working yarn is around your index finger and tail end is around your thumb and secure the yarn ends with your other fingers. Hold your palm upward, making a V of yarn (FIGURE 1). *Bring needle up through loop on thumb (FIGURE 2), catch first strand around index finger, and go

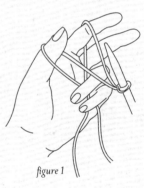

figure 1

figure 2

back down through loop on thumb (FIG-URE 3). Drop loop off thumb and, placing thumb back in V configuration, tighten resulting stitch on needle (FIGURE 4). Repeat from * for the desired number of stitches.

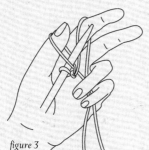

figure 3

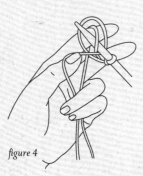

figure 4

Provisional Cast-Ons
CROCHET CHAIN PROVISIONAL CAST-ON

With waste yarn and crochet hook, make a loose crochet chain (see page 149) about 4 stitches more than you need to cast on. With knitting needle, working yarn, and beginning 2 stitches from end of chain, pick up and knit 1 stitch through the back loop of each crochet chain (FIGURE 1) for desired number of stitches. When you're ready to work in the opposite direction, pull out the crochet chain to expose live stitches (FIGURE 2).

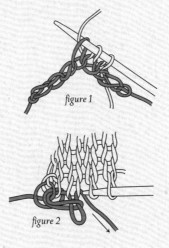

figure 1

figure 2

INVISIBLE PROVISIONAL CAST-ON

Make a loose slipknot of working yarn and place it on the right needle. Hold a length of contrasting waste yarn next to the slipknot and around your left thumb; hold working yarn over your left index finger. *Bring the right needle forward under waste yarn, over working yarn, grab a loop of working yarn (FIGURE 1), then bring the needle back behind the working yarn and grab a second loop (FIGURE 2). Repeat from * for the desired number of stitches. When you're ready to work in the opposite direction, place the exposed loops on a knitting needle as you pull out the waste yarn.

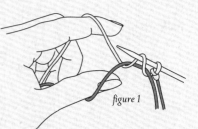

figure 1

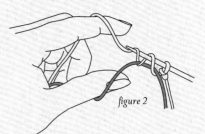

figure 2

Tubular Cast-On

With waste yarn, CO half the number of desired sts. Cont for rounds or rows as specified.

WORKED IN ROUNDS

Divide sts onto dpn, place marker (pm), and join for working in rnds, being careful not to twist sts. Cont with waste yarn, knit 2 rnds. Change to working yarn and knit 4 rnds.

NEXT RND: (RS) *K1, then use left needle tip to pick up lowest working-yarn loop from WS 4 rows below (FIGURE 1) and purl this loop (FIGURE 2); rep from * to end of rnd.

Remove waste yarn.

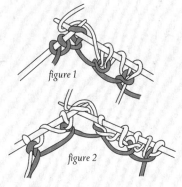

figure 1

figure 2

WORKED IN ROWS

Cont with waste yarn, knit 1 RS row, then work 2 rows even in St st (knit on RS; purl on WS), ending with a RS row. Change to working yarn and work 4 rows even in St st, ending with a RS row.

NEXT ROW: (WS) P1, *pick up lowest working-yarn loop from WS 4 rows below and knit this loop, p1; rep from * to end.

Remove waste yarn.

Crochet

Crochet Chain (ch)

Make a slipknot and place it on crochet hook if there isn't a loop already on the hook. *Yarn over hook and draw through loop on hook. Repeat from * for the desired number of stitches. To fasten off, cut yarn and draw end through last loop formed.

Single Crochet (sc)

*Insert hook into the second chain from the hook (or the next stitch), yarn over hook and draw through a loop, yarn over hook (FIGURE 1), and draw it through both loops on hook (FIGURE 2). Repeat from * for the desired number of stitches.

figure 1

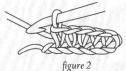

figure 2

Crochet Chain Stitch

Holding the yarn under the fabric, insert crochet hook through the center of a knitted stitch, pull up a loop, insert hook into fabric a short distance to the right, pull up a second loop through the first loop on the hook. Repeat from * as desired.

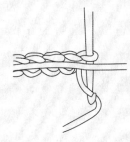

Decreases

Slip, Slip, Knit (ssk)

Slip 2 stitches individually knitwise (**FIGURE 1**), insert left needle tip into the front of these 2 slipped stitches, and use the right needle to knit them together through their back loops (**FIGURE 2**).

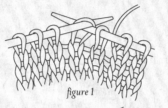

figure 1

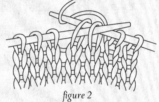

figure 2

Slip, Slip, Slip, Knit (sssk)

Slip 3 stitches individually knitwise (**FIGURE 1**), insert left needle tip into the fronts of these 3 slipped stitches, and use the right needle to knit them together through their back loops (**FIGURE 2**).

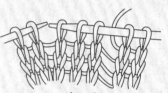

figure 1

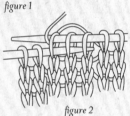

figure 2

Slip, Slip, Purl (ssp)

Holding yarn in front, slip 2 stitches individually knitwise (**FIGURE 1**), the slip these 2 stitches back onto left needle (they will be twisted on the needle) and purl them together through their back loops (**FIGURE 2**).

figure 1

figure 2

Slip, Slip, Slip, Slip, Knit (ssssk)

Slip 4 stitches individually knitwise, insert left needle tip into the fronts of these 4 slipped stitches, and use the right needle to knit them together through their back loops.

Grafting

Kitchener Stitch

Arrange stitches on two needles so that there is the same number of stitches on each needle. Hold the needles parallel to each other with wrong sides of the knitting together. Allowing about ½″ (1.3 cm) per stitch to be grafted, thread matching yarn on a tapestry needle. Work from right to left as follows:

STEP 1: Bring tapestry needle through the first stitch on the front needle as if to purl and leave the stitch on the needle (**FIGURE 1**).

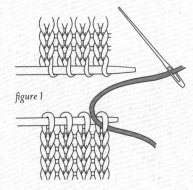

figure 1

STEP 2: Bring tapestry needle through the first stitch on the back needle as if to knit and leave that stitch on the needle (**FIGURE 2**).

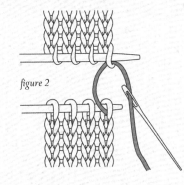

figure 2

STEP 3: Bring tapestry needle through the first front stitch as if to knit and slip this stitch off the needle, then bring tapestry needle through the next front stitch as if to purl and leave this stitch on the needle (**FIGURE 3**).

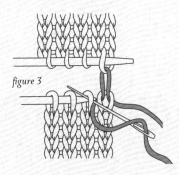

figure 3

STEP 4: Bring tapestry needle through the first back stitch as if to purl and slip this stitch off the needle, then bring tapestry needle through the next back stitch as if to knit and leave this stitch on the needle (**FIGURE 4**).

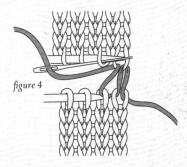

figure 4

Repeat Steps 3 and 4 until 1 stitch remains on each needle, adjusting the tension to match the rest of the knitting as you go. To finish, bring tapestry needle through the front stitch as if to knit and slip this stitch off the needle, then bring tapestry needle through the back stitch as if to purl and slip this stitch off the needle.

Increases

Bar Increase (k1f&b)

Knit into a stitch but leave it on the left needle (FIGURE 1), then knit through the back loop of the same stitch (FIGURE 2) and slip the original stitch off the needle (FIGURE 3).

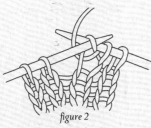
figure 1

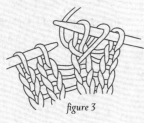
figure 2

figure 3

Raised Make-One Increase

NOTE: Use the left slant if no direction of slant is specified.

LEFT SLANT (m1L)

With left needle tip, lift the strand between the last knitted stitch and the first stitch on the left needle from front to back (FIGURE 1), then knit the lifted loop through the back (FIGURE 2).

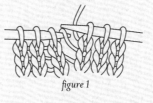
figure 1

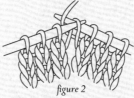
figure 2

RIGHT SLANT (m1R)

With left needle tip, lift the strand between the needles from back to front (FIGURE 1). Knit the lifted loop through the front (FIGURE 2).

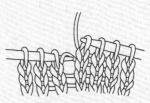
figure 1

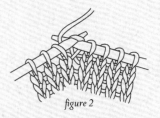
figure 2

PURLWISE (m1P)

With left needle tip, lift the strand between the needles from back to front (FIGURE 1), then purl the lifted loop through the front (FIGURE 2).

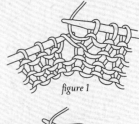
figure 1

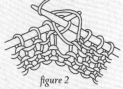
figure 2

Splicing Yarn

Overlapped Ends

Thread the end of one ball onto a tapestry needle. Leaving a couple of inches of tail, draw the needle through the end of the yarn from the other ball for a couple of inches (FIGURE 1), then exit the yarn and leave a tail hanging. Trim the tails (FIGURE 2).

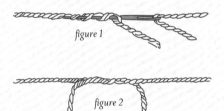

figure 1

figure 2

Wet Splice

NOTE: This method only works with yarns that are predominantly wool.

Untwist a couple of inches of yarn from each ball (FIGURE 1), then thoroughly moisten each end (saliva works best, though not always the most polite). Overlap the two ends (FIGURE 2), place them in the palm of one hand and use your other palm to vigorously rubs the ends together (FIGURE 3) The moisture and friction will cause the two yarns to felt together.

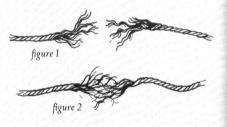

figure 1

figure 2

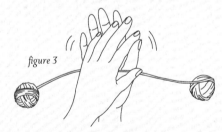

figure 3

Short-Rows

Knit Side

Work to turning point, slip next stitch purlwise (FIGURE 1), bring the yarn to the front, then slip the same stitch back to the left needle (FIGURE 2), turn the work around and bring the yarn in position for the next stitch—1 stitch has been wrapped and the yarn is correctly positioned to work the next stitch. When you come to a wrapped stitch on a subsequent row, hide the wrap by working it together with the wrapped stitch as follows: Insert right needle tip under the wrap (from the front if wrapped stitch is a knit stitch; from the back if wrapped stitch is a purl stitch; FIGURE 3), then into the stitch on the needle, and work the stitch and its wrap together as a single stitch.

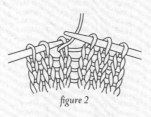

figure 1

figure 2

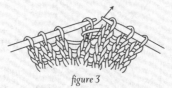

figure 3

Purl Side

Work to the turning point, slip the next stitch purlwise to the right needle, bring the yarn to the back of the work (FIGURE 1), return the slipped stitch to the left needle, bring the yarn to the front between the needles (FIGURE 2), and turn the work so that the knit side is facing—1 stitch has been wrapped and the yarn is correctly positioned to knit the next stitch. To hide the wrap on a subsequent purl row, work to the wrapped stitch, use the tip of the right needle to pick up the wrap from the back, place it on the left needle (FIGURE 3), then purl it together with the wrapped stitch.

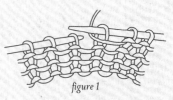

figure 1

figure 2

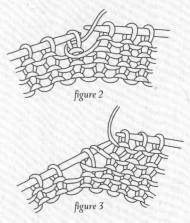

figure 3

Steeks

Use smooth waste yarn in a contrasting color to baste a cutting line along the center of the steek stitches (**FIGURE 1**). Unless a "sticky" wool yarn was used for the garment, machine-base two lines of stitches on each side of the contrasting basting yarn to ensure that stitches will not ravel. Carefully cut along the contrasting basting line for the center front (**FIGURE 2**). To finish, turn the steek stitches to the wrong side of the garment and, with yarn threaded on a tapestry needle, use a whipstitch (see below) or a series of cross-stitches to secure the facing in place.

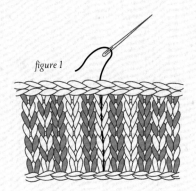

figure 1

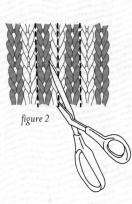

figure 2

Whipstitch

Hold pieces to be sewn together so that the edges to be seamed are even with each other. With yarn threaded on a tapestry needle, *insert needle through both layers from back to front, then bring needle to back. Repeat from *, keeping even tension on the seaming yarn.

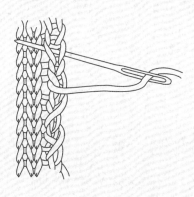

CONTRIBUTING DESIGNERS

Elinor Brown hopes to tell her grandchildren she knitted her way through medical school. She runs on good coffee, stranded knitting, and black licorice. Her designs have been published by Blue Sky Alpacas, *Interweave Knits*, *Knitscene*, *PopKnits*, *Twist Collective*, *Vogue Knitting*, and *Yarn Forward*. She writes about her knitting at ExerciseBeforeKnitting.com.

Born and raised in Philadelphia, **Jennifer Burke** has always been fascinated by color and texture. She gravitates toward textiles that utilize slipped stitches, bobbles, and cables and often finds herself incorporating bright colors and healthy doses of texture into her designs. She currently resides in Abington, Pennsylvania, with her husband, who is learning to knit.

Grace Anna Farrow learned to knit with pick-up sticks when she was in the third grade. Nowadays, she uses real knitting needles. A Philadelphia native, Grace and her family live in New Mexico, where she longs to have more seasons. You'll find her designs at astitchtowear.com.

Tanis Gray is the former yarn editor for Soho Publishing and author of *Knit Local* (Sixth & Spring, 2011). With more than 200 published knitting designs, Tanis thinks knitting is the best thing in the world. Currently residing in Washington, D.C., with her husband, son, and lazy pug, she's furiously working on her second knitting book. Check out more of her work at tanisknits.com.

Carrie Bostick Hoge lives just outside of Portland, Maine, with her husband, daughter, cats, chickens, and bunny. She has a small backyard studio where she integrates her knitting, photography, and design interests for both Madder and Quince and Company. Carrie loves her local farmer's market, food cooked from scratch, and evenings with her family. Visit her blog at swatchdiaries.blogspot.com and her website at maddermade.com.

A Shetland Island native, **Gudrun Johnston** likes to incorporate traditional Shetland knitting techniques and patterns into her contemporary designs. Using the Internet to directly interact with an international community of knitters, she has made a name for herself among a new generation of knitwear designers. In addition to self-publishing most of her designs, Gudrun has appeared in several prominent online magazines, including *Knitty.com*, *Twist Collective*, and *Knit On The Net*. For more info, visit theshetlandtrader.com.

One-half of Kelbourne Woolens and coauthor of *Vintage Modern Knits* (Interweave, 2009), **Courtney Kelley** enjoys walking her son to school every day and watching the seasons change. Her latest fall obsession is canning everything she finds in her organic garden or in the nature preserve surrounding her house. Her designs have appeared in *Vogue Knitting*, *Interweave Knits*, *Interweave Crochet*, and *Knitscene*. Courtney lives in the outskirts of Philadelphia on the banks of the Schuylkill River, with too many people in too small of a house.

Maura Kirk believes in wool in overabundance. With a BS in textile engineering, she works as a freelance designer and consultant. Her designs have been featured on the Martha Stewart craft blog and on *Knitting Daily TV*. When not knitting or crocheting, she likes to practice trapeze, ropes, and silks at her local circus school. Maura's creative pursuits are documented on her blog, theprojectoryhandcrafts.com.

Melissa LaBarre is a New England–based knitwear designer and coauthor of *New England Knits* (Interweave 2010) and *Weekend Hats* (Interweave 2011). Her designs have been published in several magazines, as well as yarn company design collections for Quince and Company, Classic Elite, The Fibre Company, and St-Denis. Visit Melissa's knitting blog at knittingschooldropout.com to see what she's up to.

Cecily Glowik MacDonald lives in Portland, Maine, with her husband, Ethan. She spends most days (and nights) knitting, designing, sizing, and writing patterns and posting on her blog Winged Knits (cecilyam.wordpress.com). The rest of her time is spent with family and friends while enjoying the beautiful coastal city she calls home.

Originally trained as an apparel and textile designer, **Laura Nelkin** learned how to knit seven years ago and has rarely touched her sewing machine since. Laura publishes knitting patterns through her company Nelkin Designs (nelkindesigns.com), teaches workshops around the country, and contributes to both print and online magazines regularly. When she is not knitting, you can find Laura on her bike, in her garden, or plotting a yummy feast with her family.

Kate Gagnon Osborn is co-owner of Kelbourne Woolens. Along with a popular line of patterns published through Kelbourne Woolens and her book co-authored with Courtney Kelley, *Vintage Modern Knits* (Interweave, 2009), Kate's designs have appeared in *Vogue Knitting*, *Interweave Knits*, and *Knitscene*, as well as in books such as *Weekend Hats*, *Knit Local*, *New England Knits*, and *The Best of Knitscene*. Kate lives in Philadelphia with her husband, daughter, and menagerie of rescued dogs and cats in an early 1900s brownstone.

Kristen Rengren is the author of *Vintage Baby Knits: More than 40 Heirloom Patterns from the 1920s to the 1950s* (STC Craft, 2009). Her designs draw on her interest in reinterpreting classic styles and are inspired by her collection of thousands of vintage knitting patterns. In addition to her work for *Twist Collective*, *Interweave Knits*, *Vogue Knitting*, and many other publications, Kristen independently

publishes her own line of vintage and original knitting patterns for women and children. You can see her work on ravelry.com or at retroknit.net, where she also peripatetically blogs about designing, vintage knitting, and making tasty jam and pie.

Jane Richmond learned the basics of knitting when she was five years old, but her love and passion evolved when she relearned as a teenager from books. She lives on Vancouver Island with her husband and began self-publishing as a creative outlet when their daughter Elsie was born in 2008. When she's not knitting, Jane blogs about knitting (among other things) at janerichmond.blogspot.com. Jane and her designs can be found online at janerichmond.com, on Etsy at janerichmond.etsy.com, or on Ravelry as JaneRichmond.

Knitwear designer and stylist **Cirilia Rose** lives in the Pacific Northwest where she is obsessed with cinema and learns lots from costumers and cinematographers alike. Happiest on set in a remote location, she can also be found in the kitchen or on the road visiting her far-flung friends. Follow Cirilia's work at bricoleurknits.com or on Twitter at twitter.com/bricoleurknits.

Cartographer by day and knitter by night, **Elli Stubenrauch** recently moved to Texas where, despite the climate, she continues to knit mittens. When she's not knitting, she enjoys genealogical research, wearing dresses,

organizing things, and playing the cello her father built for her. Her knitting patterns have been featured in a variety of publications including *Twist Collective*, *Vogue Knitting*, and *Stitch 'n Bitch Superstar Knitting*. You'll find more about Elli on her blog, *Elliphantom Knits*, at elliphantom.com.

Kristen TenDyke is a knit and crochet designer, technical editor, and author of *Finish-Free Knits* (Interweave, 2012). She lives in Maine where her days are mostly spent with yarn. When she takes a break, she enjoys exploring nature, studying healing arts and energy work, and online social networking. See more of Kristen's designs at kristentendyke.com and caterpillarknits.com.

Veera Välimäki lives in a small house in southern Finland. In addition to contributing to *Knitscene*, her knitting designs have been published by Madelinetosh Yarns and online at rainknitwear.com. Veera is interested in modern sweater designs worked seamlessly and is anxiously waiting for her small boys to learn to knit.

Melissa Wehrle holds a degree in fashion design from the Fashion Institute of Technology and worked in the industry for ten years before recently deciding to dedicate her time to her own handknit design business. She is currently working on a book with Interweave, due out in 2013. You can see more of her work at neoknits.com.

SOURCES FOR YARNS

Berroco Inc.
1 Tupperware Dr., Ste. 4
North Smithfield, RI 02896
berroco.com
in Canada: S. R. Kertzer

Brown Sheep Company
100662 County Rd. 16
Mitchell, NE 69357
brownsheep.com

Classic Elite Yarns
16 Esquire Rd., Unit 2
North Billerica, MA 01862
classiceliteyarns.com

**Fairmont Fibers/
Manos del Uruguay**
PO Box 2082
Philadelphia, PA 19103
fairmountfibers.com

Green Mountain Spinnery
PO Box 568
Putney, VT 05346
spinnery.com

Imperial Stock Ranch
92462 Hinton Rd.
Maupin, OR 97037
imperialyarn.com

**Kelbourne Woolens/
The Fibre Company**
2000 Manor Rd.
Conshohocken, PA 19428
kelbournewoolens.com

S.R. Kertzer Ltd.
6060 Burnside Ct., Unit 2
Mississauga, ON
Canada L5T 2T5
kertzer.com

Lorna's Laces
4229 N. Honore St.
Chicago, IL 60613
lornaslaces.net

Madelinetosh
7515 Benbrook Pkwy.
Benbrook, TX 76126
madelinetosh.com

Mountain Colors
PO Box 156
Corvallis, MT 59828
mountaincolors.com

Quince & Company
quinceandco.com

Schaefer Yarn
3514 Kelly's Corners Rd.
Interlaken, NY 14847
schaeferyarn.com

**Simply Shetland/
Jamieson Shetland Wool**
18375 Olympic Ave. South
Seattle, WA 98188
simplyshetland.net

Tunney Wool Company/O-Wool
915 N. 28th St.
Philadelphia, PA 19130
tunneywoolcompany.com

Westminster Fibers/Rowan
165 Ledge St.
Nashua, NH 03060
in Canada:
10 Roybridge Gate, Ste. 200
Vaughan, ON
Canada L4H 3M8
westminsterfibers.com

INDEX

Want more must-have knits to warm the season?

Don't miss these beautiful resources from Interweave.

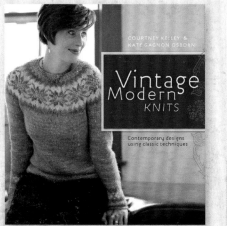

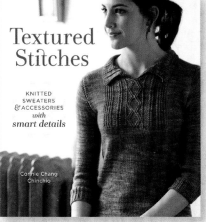

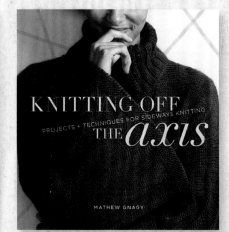

VINTAGE MODERN KNITS
Contemporary Designs
Using Classic Techniques
*Courtney Kelley
and Kate Gagnon Osborn*
ISBN 978-1-59668-240-5
$24.95

TEXTURED STITCHES
Knitted Sweaters and
Accessories with Smart Details
Connie Chang Chinchio
ISBN 978-1-59668-316-7
$24.95

KNITTING OFF THE AXIS
Projects and Techniques
for Sideways Knitting
Mathew Gnagy
ISBN 978-1-59668-311-2
$24.95

shop.knittingdaily.com

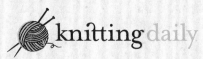

Combining a love of yarn with simple knitting has been the *Knitscene* mission since day one. Cool designs, tutorials, and photography, just like good yarn, can make your knitting lively and engaging, and is a part of every issue. Subscribe at **knitscene.com.**

Join Knittingdaily.com, an online community that shares your passion for knitting. You'll get a free e-newsletter, free patterns, projects store, a daily blog, event updates, galleries, tips and techniques, and more. Sign up for *Knitting Daily* at **knittingdaily.com.**